When We Gather
A Book of Prayers
for Worship

When We Gather
A Book of Prayers for Worship

Year A

A Collection of Worship Aids
Based on the Lectionary
Prepared for Trial Use
by the North American Committee
on Calendar and Lectionary

James G. Kirk

With art by
Corita Kent

THE GENEVA PRESS
LOUISVILLE

Material designated *BCP* is from *The Book of Common Prayer* (1977), The Episcopal Church in the United States.

Grateful acknowledgment is made to the following for the use of copyrighted material:

Doubleday & Company, Inc.: *The Jerusalem Bible,* copyright © 1966 by Darton, Longman & Todd Ltd. and Doubleday & Company, Inc.

National Council of the Churches of Christ in the U.S.A.: Revised Standard Version of the Bible copyrighted 1946, 1952, © 1971, 1973 by the Division of Christian Education of the National Council of the Churches of Christ in the U.S.A.

Oxford University Press and Cambridge University Press: *The New English Bible.* Copyright © The Delegates of the Oxford University Press and the Syndics of the Cambridge University Press, 1961, 1970.

Book Design by Alice Derr

Published by The Geneva Press®
Louisville, Kentucky 40202

PRINTED IN THE UNITED STATES OF AMERICA
9 8 7 6

Library of Congress Cataloging in Publication Data

Kirk, James G.
 When we gather.

 Includes index.
 Contents: [1] Year A—   —[3] Year C.
 1. Prayers. 2. Liturgies. I. Title.
BV250.K57 1983   264'.051013   83-14221
ISBN 0-664-24505-6 (pbk. : v. 1) (Year A)
ISBN 0-664-24553-6 (pbk. : v. 2) (Year B)
ISBN 0-664-24652-4 (pbk. : v. 3) (Year C)

To my father and mother
Roy and Helen G. Kirk
who taught me to pray

Contents

Foreword

Prayer is the soul's expression of a relationship with Almighty God. It is the bursting forth of one's conscious awareness of a God whose presence is felt. As such, prayer reveals the faith and spirituality of persons, individually and collectively, as they grope for meaning in an ever-changing world. There is a basic contemplation of Almighty God, who remains constant in one's life. There is also a thirst for quenching waters of understanding and fulfillment that arises from the inevitable rhythm of human restlessness and striving; and prayer is the outcome of that condition.

The word of God, contained in Scriptures, awakens awareness of the living presence of God, reaching out constantly toward persons in the process of becoming. All those who are spiritually attuned are moved to new openness, allowing God to expand their total being in acts of prayer. The word of God, freely given, prompts the sense of divine intervention in the life of the world. Jesus Christ, God incarnate, lived and walked among us, and suffered, bled, and died for us. One of the ways of remaining in constant touch with the living Word is through prayer. Thus, we respond spontaneously in adoration, praise, thanksgiving, confession, petition, and intercession, for our communication is with One who is alive and held dear.

Such is the life of a praying people in private and corporate worship, nourished and sustained by Scripture and continually formed by a disciplined life of prayer. Of such is the foundation of the Reformed faith.

The United Presbyterian Directory for Worship makes very explicit the fact that the initiative in all aspects of worship and praise rests with God. Prayer, an aspect of worship, is initiated by God. It undergirds all that the church does, and therefore deserves the best that is in us.

There is one major prerequisite for the pray-er, and that is the ability to "listen"—with both the inner and the outer ear. All prayer, according to the Directory for Worship, "should be guided by God speaking a gracious and correcting Word." God does not wait for human moments to determine the time to "break into" one's life. Also, God's answer to prayer is often different from the desires of the pray-er. One must develop a prayer posture, an alertness to the omniscience of God and a psychological and spiritual readiness to receive God's plaudits as well as correctives.

The prayers contained in this much-needed volume have come from the soul of a brother, beloved, one who is spiritually attuned to the "author and finisher" of all prayers. Each one flows from the word of God as though the pray-er were forced to his or her knees by the power of the Almighty. A reader approaching each prayer with openness to the movement of the Holy Spirit will become one with God as conditioned by the mood of the moment. Prayer in this volume is an assault on heaven in behalf of the world's needs.

Dr. James G. Kirk has provided not only a source book for use with lectionary readings for the day but a variety of models of prayer for use by the whole church. In addition to a spiritual depth that comes from personal faith and commitment, there is a theological depth that makes these prayers holistic in nature. Each of the forms of prayer has been sculpted by theological considerations. Listening to and for the word of God in specified Scriptures, Kirk raises and answers questions about the way God is conceived and the manner in which God intervenes in contemporary history.

The author shows a keen sensitivity to all aspects of language usage. One senses an awareness of and respect for all of humanity, as well as ease and skill in articulating such awareness. Inclusive language used in these prayers breaks down the temporary barriers of communication so often experienced in public utterances, thus facilitating oneness between God and the people, and among the people themselves.

These prayers leave no doubt in the minds of the pray-er as to where and what the "community of faith" should be and do. Through vivid metaphors, Kirk enables us to "catch a vision of God in the midst of concrete cities and abject poverty." He has skillfully merged the most basic vertical dimension of prayers with the inevitable and needed horizontal dimensions. Therefore, peacemaking in domestic and international relationships is highlighted, along with breaking down boundaries that separate people because of race, class, disability, and life-style. God's ongoing creation is seen, felt, and heard in praise and adoration by twentieth-century servants who humble themselves before the throne seeking forgiveness and guidance in order to worthily magnify the name of Jesus Christ.

This source could very well guide those who help plan for the work of the people who gather as a koinonia, seeking God at the deepest possible level. Large and small gatherings will be equally at home using these prayers as their own or as guides for developing the disciplines of mind and spirit.

JAMES H. COSTEN, *Moderator*
194th General Assembly (1982)
The United Presbyterian Church
U.S.A.

MELVA W. COSTEN, *Chairperson*
Advisory Council on
Discipleship and Worship

November 1982

Preface

Pastors spend a great deal of time preparing their sermons. Often there is very little time left to work on the other components of the liturgy. Prayers fit into that category, whether they be of praise and adoration, confession of sin, dedication of gifts, or of thanksgiving, petition, and intercession. This book is an effort to assist pastors, those participating in the liturgy, and individuals to pray in a more disciplined way.

Recently the North American Committee on Calendar and Lectionary published a lectionary for trial use. The Committee's intent was to provide Scripture readings that could be used by all the churches, thus bringing the various communions together each Sunday in the lessons being exposited. This book grew out of a desire to provide components of the liturgy based upon those readings.

The material is meant to be suggestive; it may be used verbatim; it can be adapted to meet specific needs of the congregation. Throughout, the biblical witness is evident, a witness that provides the framework for the community's praise, prayer, and guidance as it gathers to worship God.

The material is also written to be read aloud. So often public prayer is difficult to pray; the rhythm is such that more attention needs to be given to the sentence structure than to the thought conveyed. All the prayers have been read aloud in order to avoid the problem.

Throughout this material, the word "Lord" in the psalms has been retained, although it may be unsatisfactory to some people using this resource. The church needs to clarify its use of God language. Until those discussions occur, and in the absence of accepted policy, the biblical text has not been altered in regard to this term. Masculine pronouns have been altered, however. In the case of Scripture quoted from the Revised Standard Version, the inclusive word has simply been substituted; in material quoted from *The Book of Common Prayer (BCP)*, the substituted words are set off with brackets. Material from *The New English Bible (NEB)* has not been adapted to remove exclusive language because of copyright consideration. Also, material from the Revised Standard Version that has been used in the calls to worship and the litanies is not enclosed in quotation marks; the quotation marks are omitted for the convenience of the leader of worship. Unless otherwise indicated, Scripture quotations are from the Revised Standard Version.

I am indebted to loved ones and sisters and brothers in faith who read drafts of the material and offered suggestions; their enthusiasm and support provided the necessary encouragement to continue working. Corita Kent kindly agreed to provide the illustrations which highlight particular times in the Christian year. Her work has been a source of inspiration throughout my ministry, and it is an honor to have her join me in this endeavor.

I hope that what is read and used will generate a thought or two to praise God for the manifold gifts God bestows upon us. To God be all blessing, glory, and honor.

J.G.K.

Third Sunday After Epiphany, 1983

When We Gather
A Book of Prayers
for Worship

the day-spring
that we cheer

FIRST SUNDAY OF ADVENT

Lectionary Readings for the Day

Ps. 122; Isa. 2:1–5
Rom. 13:11–14; Matt. 24:36–44

Seasonal Color:
Violet

The people of God are to watch for the coming of the Lord. They are to be ready for the unexpected, and readiness takes preparation. Think of unexpected ways the Lord appears in our lives. To watch means to live in expectation. How does such anticipation affect the routine course of the day? In Noah's day a flood overtook the people and swept them away. Watch and be ready.

Call to Worship

LEADER: Come, let us go into the house of the Lord!

RESPONSE: Let us give thanks to the Lord, for that is our joyful duty.

LEADER: For the sake of sisters, brothers, and friends I will say, "Peace be within you."

RESPONSE: For the sake of the house of the Lord our God, I will pray for your good.

(Author's paraphrase)

Prayer of Confession

UNISON: God of forgiveness and mercy, hear our prayer as we confess our shortcomings and guilt. With moments so critical, we let time "just go by." With deliverance so near, we linger in the darkness. With Christ as our armor, we yet fear the unknown foe. With the night having passed, we still hesitate to greet the new day. O God, lead us forth, that the moment may be met. Dispel the shadows, so that your will may be clear. Clothed with light and new life in Christ, let us go forth as those who are awake.

Assurance of Pardon

LEADER: Jesus said that anyone who hears what he says and trusts in God has eternal life. The time is coming, indeed it is already here. All who heed God's voice shall have life.

Prayer of Dedication

O God, your will is revealed in hidden places. We are told to be ready, for your Son comes at times we do not expect. We are told to clothe the naked, feed the hungry, and visit those in prison. Quiet our fears, that we may venture confidently into the unknown and minister to strangers in our midst.

Prayer of Praise and Petition

Our eyes behold your grandeur, O God; our feet stand within the gates of your house. Prophets have sung of your mountain, where nations shall come to learn of your ways. From out of Zion your law has gone forth; out of Jerusalem has proceeded your word. Confessing you to be our judge and redeemer, we gather to give you honor and praise.

Lift us to the heights of your abode, that we may learn how to make peace here on earth. We hear of swords beaten into plowshares, yet all around lands and peoples are battered by destructive weapons. We know that our spears are not being turned into pruning hooks, but are poised to lash out at others. Turn our national obsession for security into deep concern for the safety and well-being of neighbors around the world. And grant that we may not only claim you as redeemer but serve you as agents of peace.

As Advent dawns, lead us from this courtyard of praise into paths filled with promise. Brighten our way, and help us to step out boldly in your love. When we venture into places that are hostile or strange, steady our nerves by your Spirit of truth and power. Go with us as we share with others the Advent hope.

Fill us with eagerness that waits for the dawn, curiosity that is willing to explore all truth, and impatience with injustice that refuses to leave till tomorrow the tasks of liberation. Come, Prince of Peace, in whose name we pray.

SECOND SUNDAY OF ADVENT

Lectionary Readings for the Day

Ps. 72:1–8; Isa. 11:1–10
Rom. 15:4–13; Matt. 3:1–12

Seasonal Color:
Violet

Images abound! John wears strange garments and eats uncommon food. From stones God raises children to Abraham. An ax is laid to the roots of trees that fail to bear good fruit. People will be baptized with the Holy Spirit. The wheat is gathered, and the chaff is burned with unquenchable fire. All creation serves God's mercy and judgment.

Call to Worship

LEADER: Welcome one another as Christ has welcomed you. Rejoice with one another and praise God's name.

(Author's paraphrase)

Prayer of Invocation

God of hope, fill us with the joy and peace of believing. May the power of the Holy Spirit bless what we say and do here. As Christ became a servant to fulfill your promise of salvation, so may we sing praises with our lips and serve you wholly in our lives, to the end that the nations may affirm your glory.

Prayer of Confession

UNISON: O God, you judge your people with righteousness; we judge our neighbors either right or wrong. Your Servant defended the cause of the poor; it is because of our greed that many still are poor. You bring deliverance to the needy, but we stand in the way of its being received. You send us a Savior who will crush the oppressor, but we raise up idols in his stead. Make us mindful of your dominion, how you rule while sun and moon endure. May we bow down before you and pay you the tribute that you are due.

Assurance of Pardon

LEADER: Know this: if you are willing, you will be taught. If you pause to listen, you will gain knowledge. Reflect on God's statutes and meditate on the commandments. It is God who will give insight to your mind, and your desire for wisdom will be granted.

Prayer of Dedication

The voice of one crying in the wilderness calls us to prepare your way, O Lord. Among the sounds of society you choose to reveal your will. Amid its clamor we yearn to hear voices seeking your mercy. Send us forth with clear minds so that your way is proclaimed with foresight. And grant us your benediction so that our acts are sanctified by your grace.

Prayer of Thanksgiving, Intercession, and Supplication

God of steadfastness and encouragement, you are a source of new life. When your creation moans in labor and your people cry out for compassion, you cause a sprig of hope to spring forth from a stump. You bring deliverance to the needy and justice to the oppressed. You cause your Spirit to rest on the faithful, bestowing wisdom, knowledge, and might. As a branch from the root of Jesse stands as a symbol of hope for your people, may nations respond by seeking to do your will, so that all our dwellings may reflect your glory.

Made wise by your prophets, help us to abide by your judgment. Cleansed with the water of baptism, may we not fear to confess you as our God. Not even a sparrow falls without your knowledge; may we also be mindful of your creation. You have planted in us the vision of *shalom,* when the wolf shall dwell with the lamb and none shall hurt or destroy. May we act on that dream to make peace here on earth. You send us the Christ who calls others to follow in his way; may we proclaim him the way of our lives. You assure us that you will not leave us alone; with that confidence may we become bold in our faith.

When we are confronted with poverty, give us the courage to act to free those who want. When we are aware of the lonely, let us be quick to provide comfort and companionship. When others face death, may our presence bring courage and help to fill the void. Where pain hinders movement, give us compassion to console those afflicted. As the shoot springs forth from the stump, let our actions cause it to break out into blossom, that all who hear of your love may come to rejoice with new life.

THIRD SUNDAY OF ADVENT

Lectionary Readings for the Day
Ps. 146:5–10; Isa. 35:1–10
James 5:7–10; Matt. 11:2–11

Seasonal Color:
Violet

John sends his disciples to find out if Jesus is the awaited Messiah. They are told by Jesus to report what they have seen and heard: the blind see, the deaf hear, lepers are cleansed, the poor hear good news, the dead are raised up. When John's disciples leave, Jesus tells the crowd John's identity: he is "more than a prophet," and one divinely sent to prepare the way for God's reign. The signs of that reign are already present in the midst of God's people.

Call to Worship
LEADER: Happy is the one whose help is in God.
RESPONSE: I will sing praises to God as long as I live.
LEADER: Trust in the Lord, and worship God's name.
RESPONSE: Our hope is in God, who made heaven and earth.
(Author's paraphrase)

Prayer of Praise and Adoration
You are a God of bounteous gifts, O Lord, and we bless your name. You bestow mercies without end. Your people stand upright; you give sight to the blind. You have no patience with injustice, and the meek you do not turn away. We open our hearts to your presence, and our doors to the stranger. We gather as your people, brought together by your grace and made one by your love.

Prayer of Confession
UNISON: You have taught us to be patient, and promised to supply our needs, O God. Yet we grow weary of waiting and restless with our wants. We blame our troubles on sisters and brothers, withholding from them the tolerance and care you have shown to us. O God, forgive our indulgence and help us to stand firm. In Christ you showed patience with the world in spite of the cross. Teach us to be patient, that in Christ we may have endurance in spite of our need.

Assurance of Pardon
LEADER: Know this: that we are assured of God's forgiveness, for we have a high priest set over the household of God, Jesus

Christ, the new and living way. Let us therefore make our approach in sincerity and confidence, our guilty hearts sprinkled clean, our bodies washed with pure water. The Giver of the promise is to be trusted.

Prayer of Dedication

We offer ourselves, O God, as messengers of peace and goodwill. Where war threatens and strife is real, we seek by grace to demonstrate your reconciling love. When hostilities persist and your people are alienated, our gift is Christ's promise of intercession and accord. May our words be combined with commitment to act, and our actions conform to your abiding desire.

Prayer of Thanksgiving and Commitment

You cause new life to spring forth in the desert, O God, and that which was barren to yield. By your will, waters cascade in dry places and rushing torrents subside to a flow. By your design, the crocus blooms as a sign that the winter shall end. As you have promised, weak hands are made strong, and feeble knees become firm. Those who are fearful gain boldness, the lost acquire sight of your haven. Your gifts are not exhausted by time, or depleted through use. You are a God of surprises. You are above us and beyond us, yet dwell among us. For all that you are and shall be, we give you thanks, and praise your name.

Go before us and show us your will for our lives. As in the days of Israel, give us signs of your way, a cloud by day, a fire by night. And stay behind to prod when we grow sluggish and lax. Let the prophets be heard, calling us to be faithful. Keep your commandments before us, encompassing your will. When we stumble and fall, we shall trust in Christ, our advocate, to intercede for us. He walked the path that we must walk and was obedient. He was tempted, yet did not submit. He taught us how you temper your judgment with mercy. We pray for a measure of patience as you wait at the doors of your Kingdom.

You are a generous God who gives in abundance. As you spared not yourself but came even to dwell here on earth, may we respond by giving ourselves to your service. We commit ourselves anew to the journey of faith. Make straight the highway before us as we lead your people in Christ's name.

FOURTH SUNDAY OF ADVENT

Lectionary Readings for the Day
Ps. 24; Isa. 7:10–16   Seasonal Color:
Rom. 1:1–7; Matt. 1:18–25   Violet

"Emmanuel," God with us. What a glorious gift! The words of
the prophet are fulfilled in the birth of a child. What is conceived
of the Holy Spirit and carried in Mary's womb is the promise of
eternal life to all who believe. Jesus will save God's people from
their sins; God will dwell in their midst. The Spirit makes God's
presence known now and forevermore.

Call to Worship
LEADER: The earth is the LORD's and the fulness thereof, the
           world and those who dwell therein.
RESPONSE: Lift up your heads, O gates! that the King of glory
           may come in.
LEADER: Who shall ascend the hill of the LORD? And who
           shall stand in God's holy place?
RESPONSE: Those with clean hands and a pure heart, they will
           receive blessing from the God of our salvation.
LEADER: Lift up your heads, O gates! and be lifted up, O
           ancient doors! that the King of glory may come in.

Prayer of Confession
UNISON: You shower gifts on your people, O God, and forgive
their faults. We keep accounts and settle old scores. You make
peace, sending Christ as a sign of reconciliation and hope. We
make war and call it peacekeeping. You give us a source of confidence as your Spirit is sent into our midst. We cause others to be
restless, in our anxiety and self-concern. Have mercy upon us,
forgive, and free us, that we may be renewed to serve your people
with goodwill.

Assurance of Pardon
LEADER: The Most High is called *merciful*, because God has
mercy on those who have not yet come into the world; and
gracious, because God is rich in grace to those who repent and turn
to the law; and *compassionate*, because God makes compassion
abound more and more within all of creation. Live in this knowledge, and be confident that your sins are forgiven.

Prayer of Dedication

The stage is set for the presentation of your gift of life, O Christ, and we are part of the company of players. As the curtain is about to rise, we prepare ourselves for our roles. We commit what we have to the drama that changes lives. Help us to step onto the stage with anticipation and boldness. May we know the script so well that we shall not falter as we share your gift, and ours.

Prayer of Affirmation and Supplication

O God, by your prophet you promised a sign of your presence, a son called Immanuel. And in Jesus Christ you chose to live in our midst, taste our suffering, and feel our needs. He made known your will, taught your way, and called us to follow in it. He entered the world as a tiny child, showing what dependence and promise would mean. Shepherds heard the angels' song and spread the news of the holy Child. The Magi traveled far to worship the newborn king and offer gifts. What you promised came to pass. What the prophet foretold we know now to be true.

As your story is retold and carols are sung, we hail the time appointed, and declare that your reign on earth has begun. As Jesus comes to break oppression, let us too set captives free. As he takes away transgression, let us strive for equity. We kneel in awe and wonder with shepherds and kings. As the Light of Lights descends, let us sweep away the darkness and receive the message he brings. "Watchman, tell us of the night, what its signs of promise are." Tell us of his sacrifice that banishes our terror and dread. "Come, thou long-expected Jesus, . . . born to reign in us forever." As you release us from our sins and fears, may we act to deliver your people everywhere.

O Strength and Consolation, you are the dayspring that we cheer. Yours is the time appointed; we hail the advent of your anointed One. As a woman conceived and bore for you a Son, we welcome Emmanuel, for by his birth our new life has begun.

CHRISTMAS DAY

Lectionary Readings for the Day
Ps. 96; Isa. 9:2–7

Titus 2:11–14; Luke 2:1–20

Seasonal Color:
White

A decree. A census. A man and a woman arrive in Bethlehem to obey an emperor's wish. Shepherds on the night shift tend their sheep. In the midst of these ordinary events a baby's birth is announced with extraterrestrial fanfare. Glory is given to God in the highest; peace is promised on earth. Henceforth, the world shall be enlightened by God's Word made flesh.

Call to Worship
LEADER: O sing to the LORD a new song; tell of God's salvation from day to day.

RESPONSE: For great is the LORD, and greatly to be praised; God is to be feared above all gods.

LEADER: Worship the LORD in holy array; tremble before God, all the earth!

RESPONSE: Honor and majesty are before God; strength and beauty are in God's sanctuary.

Prayer of Confession
UNISON: Your grace, O God, has appeared for the salvation of all, calling us to renounce false gods and irresponsible love. In the midst of our sin, Christ has appeared as a sign of our hope, redeeming us and calling us to be a people eager to do your will. Make us zealous for good deeds in response to your wonderful deed in Jesus Christ. We confess the vain worship of ourselves and our neglect of your children. Forgive us and empower us to live upright and godly lives in this world.

Assurance of Pardon
LEADER: Know this, that the assurance of our forgiveness has come. "For to us a child is born, to us a son is given. . . . Of the increase of his government and of peace there will be no end, upon the throne of David, and over his kingdom, to establish it, and to uphold it with justice and righteousness from this time forth and for evermore."

Prayer of Dedication
Your Word is made flesh and dwells among us, O God, full of grace and truth. For that gift and all that you bestow, we say

Alleluia and Amen! As we behold your glory, we commit ourselves to Christ's work. Make of us the body of Christ and dwell in us by your Spirit for the sake of the world that you love.

Prayer of Praise and Petition

The heavens tell of your glory, O God; all the trees of the wood sing for joy. For unto us a child is born, and into our midst has come a great light. You have come to deal justly with nations; with righteousness you rule your people. We hear of a Wonderful Counselor and know that your Spirit is near. The prophet proclaims you Mighty God, while the sea roars and fields exult. Your mercy is everlasting as you care for all your creation. We herald the Prince of Peace and await the time when his rule is complete. You are our God and are greatly to be praised. We sing unto you, honoring your name, and tell of your salvation from day to day.

Gifts have been opened and love has been exchanged. Keep us mindful that you are the source of all abundance and worth. Families have gathered and loved ones returned home. May we always remember that Christ calls us to the Table with himself as the host. The tree has been trimmed and the stockings have been hung. Let their garlands and tributes awaken assurance of your grace. Now that anticipation has given way to celebration, may we not lose sight of your continuing call to obedience and devotion.

To those who still seek a sign of your love, may we become that sign as we do justly and love mercy. To those who lack the warmth of home and friends, may we extend hospitality and good cheer. Where the sounds of war drown out Christ's call to peace, may we fulfill the tasks of reconciliation and love. You have established the world and sent the Prince of Peace. We go forth as his servants in praise of your reign!

FIRST SUNDAY AFTER CHRISTMAS

Lectionary Readings for the Day
Ps. 117; Deut. 8:1–10   Seasonal Color:
Rev. 21:1–6a; Matt. 25:31–46   White

The scene is heaven's throne; the nations are gathered. Judgment is heard as God's will is made known. There are the hungry to feed and strangers to welcome, the naked to clothe and the imprisoned to visit. The new year opens with promise; "the way of the Lord" is prepared. The call to ministry among the least of God's children is sounded.

Call to Worship
LEADER: Praise the LORD, all nations! Extol God, all peoples!
RESPONSE: For great is God's steadfast love toward us; and the faithfulness of the LORD endures for ever.
LEADER: Praise the LORD!

Prayer of Praise and Adoration
We praise your name, O God; you are glorified among the nations and in all creation. You cause the flowers to bloom; the honeycomb drips with sweetness according to your design. You dwell in teeming cities and in the quiet of the countryside. The whole earth is your habitation. You invite us into sanctuary, where we worship and bow down before you. Fill us now with your Spirit, and let your presence be our blessing.

Prayer of Confession
UNISON: You give us a vision of a world made new, O God, yet we find it so easy to abide in the old. You promise your presence among us, yet we seek so often to hide from it. We continue to mourn for our own way, though you have promised to wipe the tears from our eyes. When the former things have passed away, will we still long for what used to be? You are the beginning and the end; the middle we cling to for ourselves. We confess our nearsightedness and beg for eyes open to the new creation. May we enter the coming year made whole by your grace.

Assurance of Pardon
LEADER: Know that "the LORD your God is bringing you into a good land, . . . a land in which you will eat bread without scarcity, in which you will lack nothing. . . . And you shall eat and be full,

and you shall bless the LORD your God for the good land God has given you." God promises health and renewal. In that promise we find assurance that we are loved and accepted by God.

Prayer of Dedication

The year approaches with promise as your Kingdom is prepared, O Lord. We hear your call to ministry and offer our gifts in response. Make known your will to us as we feed the hungry, welcome the stranger, clothe the naked, and visit the imprisoned. For then we will have done these things even unto you.

Prayer of Thanksgiving and Supplication

As we cross the threshold into the new, we take time in our journey to give you thanks, O God. You have accompanied us through the year that has passed. We have been clothed and fed by your gifts. When fear has engulfed us, or we have faced the unknown, Christ our high priest has interceded on our behalf. Faced with decisions, we have been enlightened by your Spirit, and enlivened through your abiding presence. Those who have passed from our presence we have entrusted to your care. Compassion has yoked us with those ill and in pain. You are the source of all comfort and the judge of all that is done. As your commandments have served to direct our path, your discipline has kept our eyes focused on your way.

As we offer you thanks for past mercies, we seek your guidance for future tasks. In a land that abounds with resources, there are still many who are poor and without hope. Let the prophet's vision of promised abundance become real to them through our ministry. The claims of the "haves" compete for our attention and zeal; it is easy to forget those who have not. Keep us firm and insistent that it is you whom we serve, and you alone. When decisions are to be made, let us first seek your will. When we are met by challenges, stay by our side. When we enter the unknown, be our confidence and strength. And wanting for nothing, may we serve others with the fullness of new life you have promised in Christ's name.

astonished
by the
grandeur

THE BAPTISM OF THE LORD

Lectionary Readings for the Day
  Ps. 29; Isa. 42:1–9
  Acts 10:34–43; Matt. 3:13–17

Seasonal Color:
White

Jesus is baptized in order to fulfill all righteousness. When priorities are askew and directions misleading, he shows the way of God's Kingdom. When neighbors are in conflict, the Spirit descends like a dove with the hope of peace for all God's people. The baptism of Jesus portrays God's promise to set aright the creation.

Call to Worship
  LEADER: Give glory to God, worship the Lord in the splendor of holiness.
  RESPONSE: The voice of the Lord is full of power and majesty. In God's temple we cry, "Glory!"

                                       (Author's paraphrase)

Prayer of Praise and Adoration
  O God of all power and majesty, you created the heavens and stretched them out. You spread forth the earth and what comes from it. You give breath to the people and spirit to those who walk on the face of the earth. You are our Lord; glory is due your name. The former things have come to pass; we now await the new things you shall bring forth. We do indeed cry, "Glory!" as we gather to worship your name.

Prayer of Confession
  UNISON: You have given Christ as a covenant to the nations, O God, yet your people continue to live at war. Your prophets proclaim justice and peace, yet we dwell amid hostility and oppression. You judge your people with fairness; we implore you to have mercy upon us. Give sight to eyes that are blind to your truth. Enlighten our darkness, that we may behold you even in the midst of our enemies. Free us from seeking our own grandeur, so that in humility we may live at peace with your people.

Assurance of Pardon
  LEADER: The promises of God are with us still. As the prophet foretold, a Servant is sent. A bruised reed he will not break, and

a dimly burning wick he will not quench. He knows our weakness. Trust the promises of God in Jesus Christ: we are forgiven.

Prayer of Dedication

We acknowledge our baptism, O God, and the call to become members of Christ's body. Accept our gifts, that others may be led into your way. Help us so to arrange our priorities that we may seek first the reign of God on earth.

Prayer of Commitment

Your voice is upon the waters, O God. It is a voice full of power and majesty. You show no partiality; you judge the nations with fairness. You sent the message of peace to all people through your anointed one, Jesus of Nazareth. He commanded his disciples to proclaim to all the good news of reconciliation. We hear that commandment too and seek to respond. Fill us now with the same Spirit of truth. We confess before you that Jesus Christ is our Lord. As a sign of our trust in him we seek boldly to follow his way. We know that the paths of obedience and love will test us, yet we accept the risks of mission, relying on your Spirit to sustain us.

Your church, O God, has called us to be a part of the ministry of Christ. We are part of his body with a task to perform, and the gifts of Christ are ours. We join sisters and brothers in one household of faith. Let each voice be heard as worthy of trust, so that envy and suspicion will not arise. When unity is breached by alienation and strife, may the diversity of strengths keep the body intact.

In baptism you cleansed what we have been, so that we may become what you meant us to be. Let the waters of new life be poured upon our heads each day. Send down your Spirit, Lord, to infuse us with power and ignite our zeal. In all we do may you receive the glory due your name.

SECOND SUNDAY AFTER EPIPHANY

Lectionary Readings for the Day
Ps. 40:1–11; Isa. 49:1–7
I Cor. 1:1–9; John 1:29–34

Seasonal Color:
Green

John bears witness to Jesus as the one upon whom the Spirit descends. Henceforth he is known as "the Lamb of God, who takes away the sin of the world." Water is known for its cleansing power. The Spirit is recognized as the source of new life. The lamb is a symbol of innocence and faith. Rejoice in your baptism and receive anew God's merciful gifts.

Call to Worship
LEADER: I waited patiently for the Lord.
RESPONSE: God bent down to me and heard my cry.
LEADER: On my lips God put a new song.
RESPONSE: Many will be filled with awe and learn to trust in God.
LEADER: My desire is to do your will, O God; your law is in my heart.
RESPONSE: Let all those who seek you rejoice, and those who long for your saving help cry out, "All glory to the Lord!"

(Author's paraphrase)

Prayer of Confession
UNISON: Our desire is to do your will, O God; your law is in our hearts. But when misfortunes beyond counting press from all sides, and iniquities overtake us, our sight fails. When we are tempted by the vain promises of a life full of ease, our courage forsakes us and we submit to their charm. When enemies overpower us and mock our faith, we shrink back in disgrace and abandon what Christ taught. O God, we are poor and in need. You are our help and salvation. Come to our aid, and make no delay.

Assurance of Pardon
LEADER: Grace and peace is given to you in Jesus Christ. All who call upon his name he claims as his own. God will keep you firm to the end, without reproach on the Day of our Lord Jesus. It is God who called you to share in the life of God's Son, Jesus Christ. God keeps faith and forgives our sin.

Prayer of Dedication

As the Lamb of God takes away the sins of the world, we remember that we are baptized as a sign of new life. Accept these gifts, O God, which we offer as we recommit ourselves to ministry in Christ's name. May your Spirit empower us for the tasks that await, and the waters refresh us as we go forth to serve.

Prayer of Thanksgiving and Intercession

Redeemer of your people Israel, and of us, you sent your servant as a light to the nations. His salvation reaches to the ends of the earth. He taught as one with authority; his wisdom enlightens our way. He was bruised for our sakes and intercedes on our behalf. He served others as a sign of your love; he offers hope to all who are in need. You are God forever, benevolent, compassionate, and full of purpose. What you create, you leave not alone. When you judge, it is with loving concern. Those you call you also empower. Wondrous God, we come to you with thanksgiving. Incline your ear to our prayer, and look with favor on our requests.

We pray for those who are beset with burdens too heavy to bear. Draw them up out of the pits of desolation and depression, and set their feet again on solid ground. May they find in Jesus Christ a sure foundation for their lives. We pray for those who face death, and for those encumbered with sorrow at the loss of one held dear. May they rest in the conviction that you cause all pain to cease, and abide in the assurance that in Christ life shall not end. We pray for the sick and those weakened by pain. As Jesus worked wonders, making persons whole, may we in Christ's name surround the infirm with healing ministries of comfort and care. Let our comfort convince them that they do not suffer alone. Let our care provide for their dignity despite their disabling condition.

We pray for ourselves and for those offering prayers on behalf of others. Put a new song in our mouths and your praise on our lips. We delight to do your will; may your law remain in our hearts. As we speak of your faithfulness before all of your people, continue to multiply your wonderful deeds in our midst.

THIRD SUNDAY AFTER EPIPHANY

Lectionary Readings for the Day

Ps. 27:1–6; Isa. 9:1–4

I Cor. 1:10–17; Matt. 4:12–23

Seasonal Color:
Green

With a call for repentance, Jesus bids others to follow him. The message is urgent: the Kingdom of Heaven is at hand. His invitation includes the offer to make them fishers of others. The sought-for response is unconditional and unequivocal: "Immediately they left their nets and followed him." The Kingdom involves action!

Call to Worship

LEADER: Yahweh is my light and my salvation, whom need I fear?

RESPONSE: Yahweh is the fortress of my life, of whom should I be afraid?

LEADER: One thing I ask of Yahweh, one thing I seek:

RESPONSE: To live in the house of Yahweh all the days of my life.

LEADER: And now my head is held high over the enemies who surround me.

RESPONSE: So will I acclaim God with sacrifice and sing a psalm of praise to the Lord.

Prayer of Confession

UNISON: If we claim to have fellowship with Christ, yet walk in darkness, we are liars. If we claim to possess the light, but hide it under a bushel, of what use is such wisdom to the world? If we rest secure in our abundance, while all about us others go hungry and their lives are imperiled, what has become of our call to share the good news? You know our inmost selves, O God. We cannot hide from you. Forgive our betrayal of your Son, and restore us to fellowship with him.

Assurance of Pardon

LEADER: Jesus said, "I am the light of the world." Whoever follows the Christ will not walk in darkness, but will have the light of life. He has come as light into the world, that whoever believes in him may not remain in darkness. Come now to that light, for in him we are restored and forgiven.

Prayer of Dedication

Christ, you invite us to follow and become fishers of others. You equip us with talents and gifts for our venture. We humbly respond to your gracious invitation and place our gifts at your disposal. As we go out to serve, receive the results of our efforts in your name. Turn them to good where we have erred. Shed light on our path as we seek to abide in your way.

Prayer of Supplication

God of the covenant, your people who walk in darkness have seen a great light. Upon those who dwell in the night of their lives a new day has dawned. For the long-awaited Christ, whom you promised, has entered the world to illumine our way. The radiance of your glory cannot be hidden from our eyes. When we seek to live in the shadows of doubt, you reveal the folly of our ways. If the darkness of gloom overtakes us, you dazzle us with the luster of your Kingdom. Our flickering faith is matched with the brilliance of your plan for creation. We bow before you, bathed in the light of your love and aglow with the gift of your grace.

In your light may we see light, and so lead others to greater clarity of vision. Where perceptions are distorted through mistrust of Christ's message, may our lives make clear what he taught. When others are captive to seeing things only one way, let our openness provide them a choice. If because of our silence others know not what we think, give us courage of conviction and a willingness to confer. When leaders make decisions with which we do not agree, make us bold in dissent and reconciling in spirit.

Deliver us from pretension in the truth we hold; open our eyes to what others may reveal. Keep us attuned to the diversity of voices in the church, as they reflect upon your message in varied tones and accents. Lift our horizons so that we may glimpse the full scope of your covenant love. Let us dare to be astonished by the grandeur of your providence and grace.

FOURTH SUNDAY AFTER EPIPHANY

Lectionary Readings for the Day
Ps. 37:1–11; Micah 6:1–8   Seasonal Color:
I Cor. 1:18–31; Matt. 5:1–12   Green

Blessings abound for the people of God! The poor in spirit are rich; theirs is the Kingdom of Heaven. The meek inherit the earth, the merciful obtain mercy. Peacemakers are children of God, imitating their heavenly parent. And those who search for righteousness find fulfillment in their quest. In spite of persecution and slander, gladness and joy are proclaimed. For such is the nature of God's reign in our midst.

Call to Worship
LEADER: With what shall I come before the Lord, and bow myself before God on high?
RESPONSE: Shall I come with burnt offerings, with calves a year old?
LEADER: God shows you what is good; and what does the Lord require of you?
RESPONSE: To do justice, to love kindness, and to walk humbly with our God.

(Author's paraphrase)

A Litany of Confession
LEADER: When the cross appears as folly instead of God's power;
RESPONSE: Let those who boast, boast of the Lord.
LEADER: When some demand signs and others seek wisdom;
RESPONSE: Let those who boast, boast of the Lord.
LEADER: When the favored of the world claim the favor of God;
RESPONSE: Let those who boast, boast of the Lord.
LEADER: We despise the weak and long to be strong;
RESPONSE: God's foolishness is wisdom; God's weakness is strength.
LEADER: We despise the ignorant and seek to be wise;
RESPONSE: God's foolishness is wisdom; God's weakness is strength.
LEADER: We despise the lowly and struggle for status;
RESPONSE: God's foolishness is wisdom; God's weakness is strength.

An Affirmation of Blessing (UNISON)
Blessed are the poor in spirit, for theirs is the kingdom of heaven.

Blessed are those who mourn, for they shall be comforted.

Blessed are the meek, for they shall inherit the earth.

Blessed are those who hunger and thirst for righteousness, for they shall be satisfied.

Blessed are the merciful, for they shall obtain mercy.

Blessed are the pure in heart, for they shall see God.

Blessed are the peacemakers, for they shall be called children of God.

Blessed are those who are persecuted for righteousness' sake, for theirs is the kingdom of heaven.

Prayer of Dedication
We offer but a portion of the bounty you bestow, O God. Receive our gifts as we seek to walk in your way. Where justice is sought, use these gifts to bring Christ's liberating word. Where there is pain, may they bring the healing of Christ's love.

Prayer of Thanksgiving and Supplication
O God, we enter your gates with thanksgiving and come into your courts with praise. You have brought your people out of Egypt and redeemed them from bondage. You sent Moses, Aaron, and Miriam to make known your will. In Jesus Christ you portrayed the extent of your love, as he gave his life a ransom for many. He has shown us, O God, how to do justly, love kindness, and walk humbly with you.

We are taught by the psalmist to trust your will and do what is good, for then we shall be at peace with ourselves. May we be as diligent in our search for goodness as we are attentive to our desire for security.

We are also taught to commit our way unto you, since you will make our "virtue clear as the light" and our "integrity as bright as the moon" (JB). When our goodness is lessened by greed or desire, temper our wants with more moderate tastes. When our honesty is threatened by our lack of truth, make us sure of your presence so that we stand fast in our faith.

Again we are taught to wait patiently and be still, that you may speak. Quiet our longing to be like others and make us content with the word that Christ calls us as we are.

FIFTH SUNDAY AFTER EPIPHANY

Lectionary Readings for the Day

Ps. 112:4–9; Isa. 58:3–9a

I Cor. 2:1–11; Matt. 5:13–16

Seasonal Color:
Green

With a taste of salt and a glimmer of light, food is enhanced and the darkness dispelled. With life in the Spirit and the discipline of faith, neighbors are served and Christ is proclaimed. Let life find its savor in service among others, as the light of the gospel becomes a beacon of hope. Then good works shall be made manifest and God's name shall be given the glory.

Call to Worship

LEADER: Praise God. Blessed is the one who fears God and takes delight in God's commandments.

RESPONSE: Light rises in the darkness for the upright; the Lord is gracious, merciful, and righteous.

Prayer of Praise and Invocation

You are gracious, merciful, and righteous, O God. Eye has not seen, nor ear heard, nor heart conceived, what you have prepared for those who love you, yet in Jesus Christ we have a foretaste. You bring light into the darkness, causing the new day to dawn. We praise you and ask you to fill us with your Spirit.

Prayer of Confession

UNISON: You are the light of the world, O Christ, yet we do not reflect that light. You have called us salt, but our lives are bland and inspire no one. You give wisdom and the means for discerning your will. Yet we are aimless and prisoners of the whims of others. Forgive our lackluster performance as actors in your drama of salvation. Set us right and renew us by your Spirit.

Assurance of Pardon

LEADER: In the beginning was the Word, and the Word was with God, and the Word was God. In the Word is life and the life is our light. The light shines in the darkness, and the darkness has not overcome it. Know that to all who receive Christ, who believe in his name, power is given to become children of God.

Prayer of Dedication

You flavor our actions, O God, and illumine our minds. May the fruits of our labors nourish others. May the wisdom you give lead others to know Christ. May our lives be seasoned by service, and the light of our good works bring glory to your name. We have received in abundance; may we serve without ceasing.

Prayer of Adoration and Supplication

You are all-wise and all-knowing, O God; you know our thoughts before the words leave our lips. You impart wisdom and offer us the gift of new life in your Son, Jesus Christ. We have been touched by your Spirit and given a glimpse of your glory. We approach you with reverence and awe, mindful of your grace and your mercy. Look with favor upon us and grant us now a portion of your goodness, so that what we do may be your will, what we say may be good news, and who we are may be in accordance with Christ's call to be your children.

As we go forth to serve in your name, let our days reflect the brightness of your light that breaks forth like the dawn. Use us to loosen the fetters of injustice upon those oppressed by poverty, harassment, or abuse. Let us take their yoke upon us, that we may share in their burden and lighten their load. Give us the goodness to divide our plenty with those who are hungry. Free us from our love of goods and comforts so that we can take the risks and endure the rigors of service to a needy world.

Be our vanguard when opponents lie in wait before us. As Christ spoke with authority and not as the chief priest or scribes, may our witness ring true as we face the world. Save us from shrinking when we meet the slick arguments of the defenders of the status quo. Be our rearguard when we become fearful and our footsteps lag. As Christ drew away by himself when besieged by the crowds, give us the good sense also to withdraw, that we may find refreshment and rest. With the assurance that when we call you answer, and when we cry you hear us, we commit our way to you.

SIXTH SUNDAY AFTER EPIPHANY

Lectionary Readings for the Day
Ps. 119:1–8; Deut. 30:15–20 Seasonal Color:
I Cor. 3:1–9; Matt. 5:17–26 Green

The law of the Lord is not to be set aside as excess baggage. It is to be kept as a standard for appropriate behavior within God's Kingdom. Reconciliation, rather than anger, is to condition relationships; accord is to take precedence over accusation. When gifts are offered, we are to remember anything a brother or sister has against us, and first be reconciled, that we may present ourselves blameless before God.

Call to Worship
LEADER: Happy are they who conform to the law of the Lord.
RESPONSE: Happy are they who set their heart on finding God.
LEADER: A sabbath rest awaits the people of God.
RESPONSE: Let us then make every effort to enter that rest.
(Author's paraphrase)

Prayer of Praise
O God, you do call us to rest from our labors and set our hearts on finding your will for our lives. We gather in praise of your name, seeking to walk in your way. Assured of your presence, bound together by Christ, and made alive by the Holy Spirit, we worship you with our whole being.

Prayer of Confession
UNISON: God of compassion, have mercy upon us. You have given us your statutes, but we follow our own desires. We know of your laws, yet we try to justify our own way. You desire obedience, we practice rebellion. You offer blessing, we search for scapegoats. Make us mindful of how we disorder your intentions. Set us aright in accord with your design.

Assurance of Pardon
LEADER: Hear "the testimony of the Holy Spirit: he first says, 'This is the covenant which I will make with them after those days, says the Lord: I will set my laws in their hearts and write them on their understanding; . . . and their sins and wicked deeds I will remember no more at all.' And where these have been forgiven, there are offerings for sin no longer." *(NEB)*

Prayer of Dedication

Accept the gifts that we offer, O God, as we go seeking reconciliation with our brothers and sisters. In them we seek to love you with all our hearts, souls, and minds. May the reconciliation we pursue reflect our love for neighbor as ourselves. We pray in the name of the Christ who allows us to present ourselves blameless before you.

Prayer of Intercession and Supplication

O God, you are just and you treat your people with fairness. From our foremothers and forefathers we have learned your commandments: how you desired love of neighbor and not empty praise; how you called for justice and mercy rather than rites and rituals; how in our search for your justice we should show kindness, not a spirit of reprisal. We learned of Jesus, whom you sent to show us your perfect way. As he went about healing, his disciples learned of love. As he taught in the Temple, his followers heard of your promise of new life. And in his death the world would know that you are a God of infinite love. That same Jesus, whom you raised from the dead, is our chief priest, and intercedes on behalf of us all. We are strengthened by that knowledge.

We still have a distance to go in our quest of commitment and growth. Help us to learn from children what it means to have faith. May we not be afraid of dependence when it comes to trusting in you. Let us learn from our enemies what it means to forgive. May we not be so sure of ourselves that we condemn others whom you also save. Let us learn from the foreigner what it means to dwell in a strange land, and offer hospitality to the rootless, the homeless, and the estranged of this world.

Continue to nourish and sustain us, that we may mature according to your design for our lives. We are your agents in bringing others to faith. May our lives be for them an example of the confidence and endurance that come from assurance of Christ's love. May our care of and compassion toward them be a constant reminder of your abiding presence. And may our ministries to them be evidence of the fruit of an obedient life.

SEVENTH SUNDAY AFTER EPIPHANY

Lectionary Readings for the Day

Ps. 62:5–12; Isa. 49:8–13

I Cor. 3:10–11, 16–23; Matt. 5:27–37

Seasonal Color:
Green

To look with lust violates relationships. To swear an oath disguises God's mercy. The law of the Lord is a pattern against pretense. It affects how we perceive others, the relationships that we enter, and what comes forth from our mouths. The lesson is twofold: let how we behave be obedient, and let what we say have integrity.

Call to Worship

LEADER: Let your hearts wait silently for God, since God is the hope of deliverance.

RESPONSE: God alone is my rock and my salvation. I shall not be shaken.

LEADER: On God alone rests deliverance and honor. My refuge is God.

RESPONSE: Once God has spoken; twice have I heard this: that power belongs to God; and true love, O Lord, is thine.

LEADER: Let your hearts wait silently for God, since God is our shelter and strength.

(Author's paraphrase)

Prayer of Confession

UNISON: We pour out our hearts before you, O God; you are our refuge and strength. Waves of doubt beat against us, weakening our faith. Tremors of discord shake our foundation. The winds of temptations drive us from our course. Too often we rely on ourselves when wisdom is sought. Still the storms in our souls. Provide in Christ a haven of hope for our troubled and distracted spirits.

Assurance of Pardon

LEADER: Scripture declares that Christ is "a sure and steadfast anchor of the soul." He is able for all time to save those who draw near to God through him. He lives to make intercession for all. In Christ, our high priest, abides the assurance of the haven we seek.

Prayer of Dedication

O God, through your grace the foundations of faith have been laid. Christ, the cornerstone, has once and for all been set in place, and you have called us to be your building in whom the Spirit dwells. Each of us is a builder too, and in the Day of Christ our work will be revealed. Accept what we do and the gifts that we bring. May they fit your design and prove enduring.

Prayer of Thanksgiving

O God, truly you are our rock of salvation. You are the source of strength that lifts us from the depths of our own cares and concerns. We give thanks that you set our feet upon solid ground, and give us courage to face the day. The mountains you have raised as a sign of your majesty. Spring waters flow to assuage our thirst. Highways spread before us as we seek to follow your way. The cities teem with the people you have called us to serve.

We remember that you have sent us Christ as the seal of your promise. He went about healing and teaching in response to your will. When questioned by others, he relied upon you as the source of his power. Beset with doubts and fears, he was not afraid to call out your name. He withdrew from the crowds to find direction through prayer. We give you thanks that when tempted, he withstood his accuser, teaching his followers to be confident and endure.

The Holy Spirit abides with us still as a sign that you will not leave us alone, comforting and consoling us when we are distressed or in pain. The Spirit brings strength to the weak, and to the sick hope for new health. For the dying there is hospice to ease their passage into your eternal realm. The Spirit cajoles us when we are lax, and conjures up visions of your destiny for us. We give you thanks that the Spirit restores our enthusiasm and harmonizes our attempts to obey your will.

You are indeed a God of compassion and solace. We confess again and again our trust in your merciful attention to our needs. Renew us by the testimony of your enduring indulgence, and empower us through your continuing charity. With the hosts of those who have gone before us, may we go forth from this place singing your praise. We proclaim to those all about us that you are our rock of salvation!

EIGHTH SUNDAY AFTER EPIPHANY

Lectionary Readings for the Day

Ps. 119:33–40; Lev. 19:1–2, 9–18   Seasonal Color:

I Cor. 4:1–5; Matt. 5:38–48   Green

The ways of God's Kingdom demand endurance and patience. It takes endurance to resist one who is evil. Patience is needed when praying for those who would persecute. The scope of God's Kingdom is pervasive and whole. As the sun rises on evil, so rain falls on the just. Let that which we offer be in response to God's mercy, and let what we do be dependent on God's grace.

Call to Worship

LEADER: Teach us, O God, the way of your statutes;

RESPONSE: In keeping them, we shall find our reward.

LEADER: Lead us in the way of your commandments;

RESPONSE: In obeying them, we take our delight.

LEADER: Confirm in your servants your promise;

RESPONSE: And by your righteousness give us new life.

(Author's paraphrase)

Prayer of Praise and Adoration

O God, you confirm in us your promise. With the coming of Christ you have implanted your word within us, sealing the covenant once and for all. We gather to give you praise and glory. Impart to us the fullness of your truth. Lead us along the paths of righteousness in the name of Jesus, the Word made flesh, whom with you we adore.

Prayer of Confession

UNISON: It is easy to judge those who are unlike ourselves. We make them convenient targets for our own frustrations and guilt. Help us, O God, to judge ourselves aright and to show mercy to others, as we in turn look to you for mercy and forgiveness.

Assurance of Pardon

LEADER: Our assurance of forgiveness rests in Jesus, who for a short while was made lower than the angels, and was crowned with glory and honor because he suffered death, so that by God's gracious will, he should stand for us all. In him we are forgiven.

Prayer of Dedication

O God, you rule over all. The sun rises on the just and the unjust. You care for all. Let that which we offer be in response to your incredible mercy; let that which we do be dependent on your grace. Accept what we bring as signs of our endurance in faith. Lead us forth with persistence, that your way shall be known.

Prayer of Intercession

O God, you have set forth your law; we seek to obey your commandment. You have set apart a people and called them holy. We endeavor to respond to your grace, and to proclaim your glory. In Christ's name you have commissioned us to be stewards of your mysteries, bringing justice to bear where injustice prevails. We strive to serve you as ambassadors of good news, offering our labors in love to restore others to life.

Hear us as we pray for our neighbors in need. Then give us the courage to transform our words into actions. We pray for the poor, the homeless, and those who live on the streets. Protect them from those who would prey upon them, and use us to find ways to shelter and feed them. Grant that we shall not take them lightly, since you call them blessed.

We pray for those who must steal to survive. Lead us as we seek ways for society to share, so that all may live. Where systems keep persons out of work, impel us to change those systems. As we chain our doors for our protection, may we also change our ways, so that peace and security may abide in the land. We pray for those in homes, institutions, and jails. Be with those who serve them, performing their duties. Be with those who miss them, keeping their vigils of hope. Be with us who intercede on their behalf. May we seek dignity for them in spite of their condition.

O God, we will not squander your goodness or take lightly your grace. As you commission us in Christ, so empower us with the Holy Spirit that we may show ourselves trustworthy to have been set apart for your praise.

NINTH SUNDAY AFTER EPIPHANY

Lectionary Readings for the Day
Ps. 2:6–11; Ex. 24:12–18
Seasonal Color:
II Peter 1:16–21; Matt. 17:1–9
Green

Jesus took Peter, James, and John to a high mountain, and he was transfigured before them. As the season of Lent approaches, Christians remember the trial of Jesus, the meaning of his death, and the implications of his resurrection. It is a time for reflection, the season to renew commitment, and an interval when discipline may become a habit.

Call to Worship
LEADER: Worship the Lord with reverence;
RESPONSE: Happy are all who find refuge in God.

(Author's paraphrase)

Prayer of Praise and Adoration
We come with reverence to praise and adore you, O God. You have given your beloved Son for our salvation, and made the nations his inheritance, the ends of the earth his possession. You call us to be part of your household, and therein to partake of your promise. We gather as your people, attentive to your word and ready to do your bidding.

Prayer of Confession
UNISON: We seek you on the mountaintop, O God, for we fear to face the city. We would rather be dazzled by your splendor on some Sinai than obey your commands in the urban wilderness. We find it easier to worship the wonder-working Jesus than to follow the Christ, who was obedient unto death. Merciful God, forgive our shallow ways. Help us to find you wherever you choose to dwell, and to serve you wherever you choose to send us.

Assurance of Pardon
LEADER: "Since therefore we have a great high priest who has passed through the heavens, Jesus the Son of God, let us hold fast to the religion we profess. . . . Let us therefore boldly approach the throne of our gracious God, where we may receive mercy and in his grace find timely help." *(NEB)*

48

Prayer of Dedication

As the transfigured Christ revealed a life offered for the sake of us all, receive our offerings for the sake of others. Transform, O God, money into the hope for justice, time into signs of service, talents into acts of ministry, and ourselves into expressions of faithfulness.

A Prayer of Supplication

You are all-wise and majestic, O God. We approach you with awe. You set our sights on lofty heights; you stoop to hear our cries and our pleas. You spoke through your servant Moses, delivering your commandments etched out of stone. You have come with power in your Son, Jesus Christ, bringing redemption to all who believe.

We are your people, O God, called by you and commissioned to serve. We still grope for guidance in understanding our tasks. In the midst of the decisions we face, you seem so distant and removed from the scene. We need the assurance of your presence and the memory of Jesus Christ to illumine our way.

We declare our faith in the Christ as your Son with whom you are pleased. At times those words seem so empty; hearts are still hardened, and society goes its own way. Yet we cling to your promise. Help us to believe without seeing and to endure for Christ's sake even when our efforts seem fruitless.

You have sent us the Holy Spirit as our guide. We desperately need your Spirit of wisdom and truth. Help us to move with love as we seek to meet particular concerns, and to listen as long as it takes to do what is appropriate in our tangled world. May the decisions we make lead to changes that are in accordance with your will. May the care we give to our tasks reflect the care you have for your creation.

Our journey in faith goes on without ceasing. Save us from complacency with what we have done, and from fear of what you expect us yet to do. As you give meaning to our past, order and direct our present, so that the future may be shaped by your action in our lives today.

the light.
that illumines
the darkness

FIRST SUNDAY IN LENT

Lectionary Readings for the Day

Ps. 130; Gen. 2:4b–9, 15–17, 25 to 3:7   Seasonal Color:
Rom. 5:12–19; Matt. 4:1–11   Violet

Out in the wilderness Jesus is tempted. Challenged to turn stones into bread, he replies that strength comes only from God. Charged to resist the natural laws of creation, he responds that God is not to be put to the test. When invited to worship the devil in return for worldly kingdoms, he answers that God alone shall be served.

Call to Worship

LEADER: Out of the depths have I called to thee, O LORD; Lord, hear my cry.

RESPONSE: I wait for the LORD with all my soul, I hope for the fulfilment of his word.

LEADER: For in the LORD is love unfailing, and great is his power to set men free.

RESPONSE: I wait for the LORD with all my soul, I hope for the fulfilment of his word.

(NEB)

Prayer of Praise and Adoration

You have the power, O God, to set all captives free. In Jesus Christ you have sent your liberating word into the world, breaking the fetters that enslave your people. Make us attentive to the good news of redemption proclaimed in our midst, as here we worship and adore you.

Prayer of Confession

UNISON: When confronted by temptations, we are easily overcome. They allure us with promises we find hard to resist. We harbor fantasies of how our lives might have been. Our dreams become pervasive, hiding the truth of your love. O God, have mercy upon us; enable us to discern deception when it appears. Enlighten us to your genuine renewal in Christ.

Assurance of Pardon

LEADER: "It was clearly fitting that God for whom and through whom all things exist should, in bringing many sons to glory, make the leader who delivers them perfect through sufferings.

. . . For since he [Christ] himself has passed through the test of suffering, he is able to help those who are meeting their test now." *(NEB)*

Prayer of Dedication

God of compassion, you minister to us in our wilderness. When barren wastes surround us, you hear our prayers of petition. In times of want, you ease our plight with mercy. In times of plenty, all that we have comes from your grace. In bringing our gifts to you, we return what is already yours. May these gifts be used to bring all your people into the promised land.

Prayer of Supplication

O God, we stand before you shorn of all pretense and pride. If we boast, it is because of your grace. What goodness we have, you have bestowed upon us. You created us and gave us our name. As a fine potter works the clay, so have you fashioned us. You shape us and mold us to fit your design. Out of the depths we cry unto you, our maker; hear our voice and be attentive to our supplication.

When we are cast into the wilderness and alone with ourselves, keep us from temptation beyond what we can endure. As in the garden you provided all that man and woman needed, so now let us rely on your goodness to protect us from harm. We are tempted to turn your blessings into means to gratify ourselves. Money, status, and power seduce us. Teach us the mind of Christ, who emptied himself and took the form of a servant. And when others treat us with disdain, and their taunts wound us and weaken our resolve, keep us firm in our confession that it is your favor we seek. When success comes our way, and friends speak well of us, help us to receive these gifts as the ministry of your angels, and praise your name without ceasing.

Bring us back from times alone better equipped to serve the needs of others. In Jesus Christ the free gift of your righteousness has come to us. Use us in turn to set upright those lives that are askew. Empower us to bring comfort to those who mourn, wholeness to those who are sick, the bread of life to the hungry, and the cup of salvation to the oppressed. Help us to give from the abundance of the blessings you bestow, so that others may abound in your promise of new life.

SECOND SUNDAY IN LENT

Lectionary Readings for the Day
Ps. 33:18–22; Gen. 12:1–4a, (4b–8)   Seasonal Color:
Rom. 4:1–5, (6–12), 13–17; John 3:1–17   Violet

John's Gospel speaks of rebirth and new life. Both are required to enter God's Kingdom. Rebirth occurs as one is baptized, receiving God's Spirit. New life is received through God's gift of God's Son. It is time to put the old order aside in order that God's will may be known. Baptism and repentance remain points of departure for life lived in faith.

Call to Worship
LEADER: Behold, the eye of the Lord is on those who fear God, on those who hope in God's steadfast love.
RESPONSE: Our soul waits for the Lord; God is our help and shield. Yea, our hearts are glad because we trust in God's holy name.
LEADER: Let your steadfast love, O Lord, be upon us, even as we have put our hope in you.

(Author's paraphrase)

Prayer of Praise and Adoration
You keep your eye upon us, O God; you protect us as a shield. You give us hope in spite of the disquiet that lingers within us; you lift our spirits and make us glad. All creation sings your praise; we your people laud your name. Hear us as we worship, and speak to us as we gather. For we seek to be filled with your Spirit and made alive by your abiding Word.

Prayer of Confession
UNISON: You call us to become pilgrims, to follow you in a journey by faith. We would find it easier to follow when not so much is at stake. But you promise that you will be with us and that our needs will be met. We cling to our possessions, trusting in them for security. You lead us into unfamiliar places, asking that we trust in your will. O God, your way is challenging when we choose to be complacent. You make great demands; we are anxious and uncertain. Have mercy upon us and forgive our hesitant steps toward the promise.

Assurance of Pardon

LEADER: "Jesus . . ., for the sake of the joy that lay ahead of him, endured the cross, making light of its disgrace, and has taken his seat at the right hand of the throne of God" *(NEB)*. Our faith depends on him from start to finish, and he unceasingly intercedes on our behalf. Therein lies our hope and our assurance.

Prayer of Dedication

O God, you have sent your Son into the world, that we may have life. As we go forth from your sanctuary, may we offer that life in Christ's name to our neighbor. Use our talents to build up Christ's body. Use the money that we give to bring healing for his sake. All that we give is in response to your benevolent care.

Prayer of Supplication

You reckon us righteous, O God, in accordance with your covenant made long ago and fulfilled in Jesus Christ. You promised to the descendants of Abraham and Sarah the righteousness that comes by trusting your will. You have sent Jesus Christ as the guarantor of our hope, since he was faithful to you in all ways. You seal our inheritance at baptism in Christ's name, as a sign of our cleansing by your grace. In company with all those whom, down through the ages, you have called as the people of faith, we give you thanksgiving and the honor due your glorious name.

As we continue our journey in quest of your promised land, send your Spirit to accompany us as a source of guidance and strength. We fear to leave the security we have gained. Decisions are not easy when our own comfort is at stake. Send your Holy Spirit to give us courage and the clarity we need. We carry with us a heavy burden of past failure and present guilt. Send your Holy Spirit to assure us of your acceptance and forgiveness in Christ, so that, relieved of our own burden, we may ease the burden of others. The demands of the gospel lead us into paths unknown; we fear the risk. Our hope quickly fades; our confidence wanes. May the Holy Spirit give us the boldness we need.

Abraham, Sarah, and Lot left their homeland, as you bade them to do. We follow their example as your children called by Christ. Look with favor upon us as we seek to walk boldly in faith. May our journey be charted according to your design, and the course that we follow be in line with the path Jesus walked for our sake.

THIRD SUNDAY IN LENT

Lectionary Readings for the Day

Ps. 95; Ex. 17:3–7

Rom. 5:1–11; John 4:5–26, (27–42)

Seasonal Color:
Violet

True worship is not confined within the walls of a sanctuary; nor is it limited to certain times and seasons. Jesus speaks of worshiping God in spirit and in truth. God's people bear witness to the indwelling Spirit in all that they do. The truth that guides them is substantiated through acts of forbearance and love. May all that is done praise God's name!

Call to Worship

LEADER: O come, let us sing to the LORD; let us make a joyful noise to the rock of our salvation!

RESPONSE: Let us come into God's presence with thanksgiving; let us make a joyful noise to God with songs of praise!

LEADER: O come, let us worship and bow down, let us kneel before the LORD, our Maker!

RESPONSE: For we are God's people, the flock that God shepherds. We shall know God's power if we listen to God's voice!

Prayer of Confession

UNISON: Do not harden our hearts, O God, to the sound of your voice. We confess we don't listen to the word that you send. You give us Jesus, the Word of life in our midst. We confess our delay in obeying the direction he brings. You promise the Holy Spirit, a source of counsel and power. We confess ignoring such guidance, since we do not respond. Forgive us our sin, and help us through Christ to enter the rest you have promised.

Assurance of Pardon

LEADER: "Therefore, now that we have been justified through faith, let us continue at peace with God through our Lord Jesus Christ, through whom we have been allowed to enter the sphere of God's grace, where we now stand. . . . But that is not all: we also exult in God through our Lord Jesus, through whom we have now been granted reconciliation." *(NEB)*

Prayer of Dedication

Just as our worship of you, O God, is not confined to this place, so also our praise is not limited to certain times or seasons. Accept the offerings that we bring as a witness to your Spirit, who dwells in all that we do. May our acts of forbearance and love testify to Christ's truth pervading our lives. Use what we give so that others may come into your presence with joyful songs of thanksgiving and hope.

Prayer of Thanksgiving and Petition

O God, at Horeb you caused water to come forth from a rock. At Sychar, Jesus came to drink from Jacob's well. When throats have been dry or your people have felt parched, you have led them to streams of your kindness, bringing refreshment and new life. We have taken that water and set it apart in Christ's name, knowing that in him we need not ever thirst again. Cleansed of our sin and justified by Christ's faith, we receive the promise of your grace. Given new hope of sharing your glory, we come before you with thanksgiving, as the source of our having been washed and set apart as Christ's church.

Hear our prayers for all those who feel pain; may they persevere with greater patience and strength. May our arms enfold them as we support them in their trials. May our presence be of comfort as we bear with them their dis-ease. We have heard that endurance develops character. May we through our mutual forbearance as sisters and brothers learn what it means to trust in your love. Having sent us your Son, who himself agonized with death, you have shown us to what extent you will go to relieve estrangement and distress. With our lives attuned to your purpose and will, may we be of some hope to those needing your word. And may that word be one of reconciliation as they are enabled in Christ to find peace in your care.

Give us faith, O God, like that of Moses at Horeb. Let us not be among those who would put you to the test. Rather, trusting in Jesus who invites us to drink from the well of eternal life, may we draw from that source as we offer the cup to our neighbor in need.

FOURTH SUNDAY IN LENT

Lectionary Readings for the Day

Ps. 23; I Sam. 16:1–3   Seasonal Color:
Eph. 5:8–14; John 9:1–41   Violet

The man blind from his birth receives sight as a gift. Arguments occur concerning the cause of his healing. Did Jesus profane the sabbath? Was the man's blindness due to his birth in utter sin? In the midst of the turmoil the man believes and worships the Christ. Truly, there are those who see but behold not the truth. Christ comes that all may discern God's mercy and grace.

Call to Worship

LEADER: The LORD is my shepherd; I shall not be in want.
RESPONSE: You spread a table before me in the presence of those who trouble me;
LEADER: You have anointed my head with oil, and my cup is running over.
RESPONSE: Surely your goodness and mercy shall follow me all the days of my life,
UNISON: And I will dwell in the house of the LORD for ever.
(BCP)

Prayer of Praise and Adoration

Shepherd God, you caused your Spirit to come mightily upon David. You promised your children your comforting presence and direction. You sent Jesus as the light of the world to remove the scales from our eyes. We behold your grandeur and offer the praise due your name.

A Litany of Confession

LEADER: For once you were darkness, but now you are light in the Lord.
RESPONSE: May Christ give us the light, that we may awaken to his truth.
LEADER: Walk as children of light as you pursue what is good, right, and true.
RESPONSE: May Christ give us the light, that we may awaken to his truth.
LEADER: Take no part in works of darkness but try to learn what is pleasing to God.

RESPONSE: May Christ give us the light, that we may awaken to his truth.

Assurance of Pardon

LEADER: Jesus has said, "As long as I am in the world, I am the light of the world. . . . For judgment I came into this world, that those who do not see may see, and that those who see may become blind." As we confess our sins to God in Christ's name, he intercedes on our behalf as we are awakened from death to the hope of new life.

Prayer of Dedication

As you pray for us in spite of our wayward behavior, O Christ, so also we intercede for others with the assurance of new life for them. Translate now our prayers into acts of charity and peace as we offer these gifts. Let us not be content with our giving while others live a life less than fulfilled.

Prayer of Supplication

You, O God, the Good Shepherd, lead your people along still waters. You have sent your Son, Jesus Christ, into the world as the lamb who redeems your people from their sin. He has become the light that illumines the darkness, allowing us to learn what is pleasing in your sight. You know the thoughts of our hearts before we speak. Hear us then as we utter this prayer.

As you lead us along paths of righteousness, give to us the clarity of vision to discern the way we should go. Our spirits are eager to be faithful in Christ's name. The problems that confront us impel us to act. When we hold back for fear that we will fail, may your Spirit infuse us with the courage to proceed. The issues that face us often do not lend themselves to simple solutions. May your rod and staff comfort us with the promise of your presence. There are many who hunger for sustenance, and thirst after their own redemption from the demons that enslave them. May we take from your table the bread that will nourish them with the truth of your gracious salvation; may we lift to their lips the cup that holds the promise of new life.

Your goodness and mercy dwell with us throughout our lives. As members of your household we inherit the promise of your rest. Help us in times of reflection to discover the truth, and in times of action to be more decisive and deliberate. As we pass through valleys that await us, may we be led by your radiance and refreshed by the promise that you shepherd us still.

FIFTH SUNDAY IN LENT

Lectionary Readings for the Day

Ps. 116:1–9; Ezek. 37:1–14

Rom. 8:6–11; John 11:(1–16), 17–45

Seasonal Color:

Violet

Lazarus is dead, and Jesus weeps with compassion. Approached by Martha and Mary, he translates concern into action. He goes to the tomb, and from thence Lazarus steps forth. The one who was dead is unbound and set free. Jesus' ministry abounds with accounts of those likewise released from bondage. He was and continues to be a merciful high priest on behalf of God's people.

Call to Worship

LEADER: Gracious is the LORD, and righteous; our God is merciful.

RESPONSE: I walk before the LORD in the land of the living.

Prayer of Praise and Adoration

You are merciful and just in the deliverance of your people, O God. You draw us up out of the depths of distress; you incline your ear as we call on your name. Our souls rest in you and in the promise of Christ's redeeming love. Lay now your hand upon us, and draw us out by your Spirit, that we may sing praises to your name.

Prayer of Confession

UNISON: You called us to life in the Spirit, yet we seek to satisfy the flesh. We call you gracious, yet we practice greed. We praise you with our lips, O God, yet we do not honor you in our lives. Discontent consumes us as we yearn for still more things. We know that to live by your grace promises inheritance of new life. Redeem our enslavement to corruptible desires, that we may be worthy to be called righteous in Christ.

Assurance of Pardon

LEADER: Paul declares that if the Spirit of God dwells in us, the one who raised Christ Jesus from the dead will give life to our mortal bodies through God's Spirit which dwells in us—for all who are led by the Spirit of God are children of God. Believe this word of promise and walk in newness of life.

Prayer of Dedication

O God, as Jesus released Lazarus from the hands of death, may our ministry give to others the promise of new life. Accept the gifts that we offer to proclaim your love. Use our talents in ways that will set others free. May the liberating truth of Christ's gospel be heard anew in the land.

Prayer of Thanksgiving and Petition

O God, you rob death of its sting; you cause graves to set free their captives. You assemble and enliven dry bones strewn amid barren fields. Through the grace of the Holy Spirit sent forth in Christ, our mortal lives are aflame with your presence and redeemed by your love. You hear the voice of our supplications, inclining your ear to our needs. We give you thanks for your indulgence, your kindness and care. We owe our lives to your righteous salvation in the gift of your Son. We are the people of your compassion, your judgment, and your justice. You are our God and we give you the praise due your name.

Hear our prayer for those bones that have become brittle and dry. We pray for the aging, those in our midst whose movements are not so swift as they once were. May the breath of life that you give them be for us an abiding source of inspiration and wisdom. Give to us patience to listen to what they say, and may our presence be for them a comfort as they meet each new day.

Hear our prayer for those whose muscle lacks sinew and is no longer pliable or tight. We pray for the lazy and those who are overly cautious when called upon to act. Give to them a discipline that will train them in faith, and may we show them a boldness tempered with patience and care. Hear our prayer for those whose flesh is different from ours because of pigment and race. We pray for sisters and brothers of all colors who give radiance to Christ's church. Assemble our diverse gifts in a vivid display of our common baptism in Christ, and set ablaze the unity of our witness with the Holy Spirit, who binds us as one. So breathe on us, breath of God, and fill us with life anew, that we may love what you love, and do what you would do.

PASSION SUNDAY/PALM SUNDAY

Lectionary Readings for the Day
Ps. 31:9–16; Isa. 50:4–9a
Phil. 2:5–11; Matt. 21:1–11

Seasonal Color:
Violet

Garments and branches were spread on the road. The way was prepared, fulfilling the promise of Scripture. The king indeed came "on a colt, the foal of an ass." Amid shouts of "Hosanna" and blessings, the prophet of Nazareth entered Jerusalem, acclaimed as a king. As the streets were cleared and the cheering subsided, a drama unfolded that even today grips the hearts of the crowds.

Call to Worship
LEADER: Open to me the gates of righteousness,
RESPONSE: That I may enter through them and give thanks to the LORD.
LEADER: I thank thee that thou hast answered me and hast become my salvation.
RESPONSE: This is the LORD's doing; it is marvelous in our eyes.
LEADER: This is the day which the LORD has made;
RESPONSE: Let us rejoice and be glad in it.

Prayer of Praise
You give us tongues to speak comforting words to those who are weary. Each morning you awaken us to the words of new life. Open our ears that we may hear of your redemption; open our lips that we may confess Christ as the source of all righteousness and faith. Our time is in your hands, O God; we give you praise for your goodness that has no end.

Prayer of Confession
UNISON: O God, we confess our distress when afflicted with pain. We often avoid those encounters that will cause us discomfort. It is easier to hide from distress than to be exposed to forms of misery and grief. Yet we believe in Christ, who was sacrificed for all. Help us to trust in him when he calls us to bear abuse on his behalf.

Assurance of Pardon
LEADER: Our assurance of pardon is in Jesus, "who, though he was in the form of God, did not count equality with God a thing

to be grasped, but emptied himself, taking the form of a servant . . . and became obedient unto death . . . on a cross." Through his obedience we are freed from whatever bondage enslaves us.

Prayer of Dedication
Blessed is the one who comes in the name of the Lord. Blessed are the gifts that are received in Christ's name. We come before you, O God, with the many blessings that you have bestowed upon us. Accept them as in Christ you accept us. Use what we bring, so that others can shout, "Hosanna, Christ reigns!"

Prayer of Thanksgiving and Petition
O God, we give thanks for your Son Jesus, whom we confess as our Lord. You sustain us by his word when we grow weary in faith. You have caused your commandments to pervade his life, giving focus and direction to our attempts to obey your will. When we stumble and fall, it is he who intercedes on our behalf. He is our righteousness and redeemer, our source of hope and the anchor of our assurance. He suffered rejection and endured the cross. We approach you with boldness, with acceptance through his promise of new life. He is indeed the name above every name, the one who enables and frees our tongues to confess, to give you all glory as God of our lives.

May our thanksgiving breed endurance as we offer our lives to others in Christ's name. There are those whose energies are sapped by sorrow, whose bodies are bent with grief. Imbued with your Spirit, we seek to infuse them with hope. There are others who are scorned by their neighbors, cast aside as being inferior or of no use. We are encouraged by the forgiveness you give us in Christ; let our words of acceptance offer them asylum and rest. We hear whispers of gossip, and are witness to plots that will repay still others for wrongs that they have done. Let us at those times be emboldened to speak the word of reconciliation and peace.

Keep us from compounding the pain that is inflicted on your people by whatever cause. Christ made the sacrifice once and for all. May we in Christ's name have compassion on all those who suffer abuse, joining with them in the one hope that makes all things new.

fullness

of joy

THE RESURRECTION OF THE LORD
EASTER DAY

Lectionary Readings for the Day
Ps. 118:14–24
Acts 10:34–43; Col. 3:1–4; John 20:1–18

Seasonal Color:
White

Mary's Easter Day was a mixture of discovery, sadness, and awareness. With her discovery she runs quickly to tell the others. In her sadness she finds comfort among the angels. When made aware of Jesus' presence she calls him "Rabboni," teacher. Easter continues today as a time to relate the good news, to find comfort, and to confess Christ as the source of new truth.

Call to Worship
LEADER: Christ is risen!
RESPONSE: Christ is risen indeed!
LEADER: This is the day which the LORD has made;
RESPONSE: Let us rejoice and be glad in it.

Prayer of Praise and Adoration
This is indeed the day which you have made, O God, a day of gladness and rejoicing. You cause new life to burst forth with great beauty and fragrance. You adorn the creation with splendor and grandeur. You give your people a taste of your righteousness as we worship the Christ, the cup of new life. Be with us now as we enter the gates of your temple, and hear us as we give you thanksgiving and praise.

Litany of Assurance
LEADER: With the stone rolled away came emptiness
RESPONSE: Of a tomb that held captive the Crucified,
                 of the space that was once filled with death,
                 of the cross that now pointed to greater truth
                 of God's love in spite of ourselves.
LEADER: With the stone rolled away came questions
RESPONSE: From those whose world lay shattered,
                 from those who would demand living proof,
                 from those who were seeking a sign of promise
                 breeding confidence, assurance, and trust.
LEADER: With the stone rolled away came light
RESPONSE: To illumine the darkness of suspicion and fear,
                 to dispel the shadows of distrust, anxiety, insecurity,

to radiate with the beams of new hope and understanding
the life about to be lived.
LEADER: With the stone rolled away comes a future
RESPONSE: With a truth that outshines the wisdom of ages,
with space to be filled with the Kingdom of God,
with the company of those who through history
confess
Jesus Christ is risen today. Alleluia! Amen.

Prayer of Dedication

O God, we come with our offerings in response to your love.
With the new life in Christ, we give ourselves in service to others.
With the energy bestowed by the Spirit, we seek to inflame all
your people with a zeal for your way. Receive the work we do,
and the gifts we bring, that they may become a blessing in your
sight.

A Prayer of Thanksgiving

All honor, praise, and glory are due your name, O God. You
are God who causes the breath to fill our lungs, our eyes to see,
and our lips to proclaim your merciful name to all the nations.
You awaken us this day with the dawn of a new age, with the
sun rising on friend and foe alike, and the truth of Christ's redeeming resurrection ablaze across the heavens. Christ is risen
indeed to bring fullness of life to all your people.

We give you thanks that in Christ Jesus you reveal to us your
Word. As prophets listened to your voice, make us likewise attentive to the Word that became flesh, and thereby empowered
to speak the truth of your love.

We give you thanks that in Christ Jesus you have opened the
way for all to approach you in prayer. As he offered himself as
a sacrifice that was pleasing in your sight, we yearn for the day
when all that we do will be in praise of your name. We confess
Christ as the cornerstone of the church. As we seek to respond
to his call, may our conviction breed courage, and our charity
challenge others to approach you with hope.

We give you thanks that even now in Christ Jesus we taste the
new wine of the gospel. Already the past is finished and gone. We
gather this day as the community of witnesses to the meaning of
Jesus for all human life. Fill us with the Spirit of the resurrection
as we seek to become your redemptive society.

SECOND SUNDAY OF EASTER

Lectionary Readings for the Day
Ps. 16:5–11
Acts 2:14a, 22–32; I Peter 1:3–9;   Seasonal Color:
John 20:19–31   White

"The peace of the Lord be with you." Jesus died that all may
henceforth have life. "The peace of the Lord be with you." He
sent forth his people to serve. "The peace of the Lord be with
you." Jesus said his people would receive God's Spirit. The truth
of the gospel is contained in the peace of God.

Call to Worship
LEADER: O LORD, you are my portion and my cup, it is you
who uphold my lot.
RESPONSE: My boundaries enclose a pleasant land; indeed, I
have a goodly heritage.
LEADER: I will bless the LORD who gives me counsel; my heart
teaches me, night after night.
RESPONSE: My heart, therefore, is glad, and my spirit rejoices;
my body also shall rest in hope.
LEADER: You will show me the path of life; in your presence
there is fullness of joy.   *(BCP)*
RESPONSE: Let us worship God!

A Litany of Assurance
LEADER: By God's great mercy we have been born anew to a
living hope through Christ's resurrection from the
dead.
RESPONSE: This Jesus God raised up, and of that we all are
witnesses.
LEADER: We have an inheritance which is imperishable, un-
defiled, and unfading.
RESPONSE: This Jesus God raised up, and of that we all are
witnesses.
LEADER: By God's power we are guarded through faith for a
salvation to be revealed in the last time.
RESPONSE: This Jesus God raised up, and of that we all are
witnesses.
LEADER: The trials you may suffer are so that your faith may
prove itself worthy of all praise, glory, and honor
when Christ is revealed.

RESPONSE: This Jesus God raised up, and of that we all are witnesses.

LEADER: As the outcome of your faith you obtain the salvation of your souls.

RESPONSE: This Jesus God raised up, and of that we all are witnesses.

(Author's paraphrase)

Prayer of Dedication

You promise your peace through the gift of your Son. Alive with your Spirit, O God, we are sent forth to serve. We offer you now the firstfruits of our labor. Accept them and use them in accordance with your desires.

Prayer of Thanksgiving and Petition

All blessing and honor is due unto you, O God; by your unending love we have been born again to a life full of freedom and hope. You have caused the bonds that enslaved us to be loosened through your forgiveness offered in Christ Jesus. You have opened our eyes through his vision of your gracious will. We see now what it means to care for our neighbor. With his sacrifice made once and for all you broke down the walls of enmity and strife. We are able to cross lines of hostility, seeking reconciliation and peace. For all that we thank you, as we offer this prayer.

We thank you for the life full of freedom and hope. We pray that what we do will be worthy of your covenant that Christ sealed on the cross. We thank you for forgiveness which opens our eyes to your gracious will. We pray that you will pour out your Spirit freshly upon us, and kindle us anew with the flame of your desires. We thank you for neighbors, and for showing us what it means to care. We pray that as we prophesy, you will give us commitment to act within your society. We thank you for breaking down the walls of enmity and strife. Let us not be content with the way things are, when so many are suffering without some sign of hope. We thank you for the ability to cross lines of hostility, seeking reconciliation and peace. As we see visions of what ought to be done, make us not afraid to speak out on behalf of those whose voices are not heard. We thank you for Christ who suffered on behalf of us all. When our faith is put to the test, and we face the trials that obedience demands, fill us with boldness to proclaim just what new life may mean.

THIRD SUNDAY OF EASTER

Lectionary Readings for the Day
Ps. 116:12–19
Acts 2:14a, 36–41; I Peter 1:17–23;   Seasonal Color:
   Luke 24: 13–35   White

Two men on the road to Emmaus encounter another who appears to be a stranger. They relate to him what has happened, how Jesus was tried and sentenced to death. In response he tells them how it was necessary to accomplish what the Scriptures foretold. At table that evening his identity was revealed as he took bread and blessed it. The extent of God's love becomes known each time bread is broken and shared. The truth of God's mercy remains; Christ has risen indeed!

Call to Worship
LEADER: I will fulfill my vows to the LORD in the presence of all [God's] people.
RESPONSE: I will offer you the sacrifice of thanksgiving and call upon the Name of the LORD.
LEADER: In the courts of the LORD's house, in the midst of you, O Jerusalem, let us praise God.

(BCP)

Prayer of Praise and Adoration
We enter your courts with praise, O God; we come into your house with thanksgiving. In Christ you give us the cup of salvation; in him we receive the bread of life. To you indeed our vows are to be made; you shall hear our confession of faith. So be with us now as we gather, and be pleased with the homage we bring.

Litany of Affirmation
LEADER: You know that you were ransomed from futile ways with the precious blood of Christ.
RESPONSE: That word is the good news preached to you.
LEADER: He was destined before the foundation of the world but was made manifest at the end of all times for your sake.
RESPONSE: That word is the good news preached to you.
LEADER: Through him you have confidence in God, who raised him from the dead and gave him glory.
RESPONSE: That word is the good news preached to you.

LEADER: Having purified your souls by your obedience to the truth, love one another earnestly from the heart.

RESPONSE: That word is the good news preached to you.

LEADER: You have been born anew, through the living and abiding word of God.

RESPONSE: That word is the good news preached to you.

Prayer of Dedication

We bring our gifts to you in response to good news. Christ is risen indeed and abides in us still. May all that we do be in response to new life. As you accept who we are, O God, receive what we offer, and transform all of our being to conform with your will. Extend your grace through us so that others hear of the salvation you bring.

Prayer of Thanksgiving and Petition

O God, we are a people of promise, thanks to your abiding grace. Through the gift of your Son Jesus we are born anew. You do not forsake us when we stray from your way. You have sent us the Christ, who shows us your will. In our distance from you he has redeemed us from exile, and been by our side. He brings us the light to illumine your desires, and shows us our error when we disobey you. In him we have confidence that you will set things aright. For all that we thank you through Christ.

We pray for all who have their own Emmaus to reach, whose eyes have not seen that Christ lives in their midst. We pray for those who fear losing control of who they shall be. Help us to show them what it means to be filled with the Spirit. We pray for those seeking to cope with the pressures they face. Help us to guide them to submit to your will. We pray for those who fashion idols of what Christ ought to be. Help us to teach them how to obey his commands. Help us to guide them to take that first leap of faith. May they discover through their trust that you do not leave them alone.

There are others who have heard the good news and now wonder what it means. They are new to Christ's church and eager for faith. They are tempted to be overzealous and expect results beyond their means to accomplish. Help us, O God, to surround them with care. While we partake of their zeal, may we temper their desires, and together grow in fulfilling Christ's call. While our hearts burn within, open the Scriptures to us.

FOURTH SUNDAY OF EASTER

Lectionary Readings for the Day
Ps. 23

Acts 2:42–47; I Peter 2:19–25; John 10:1–10

Seasonal Color:
White

Jesus teaches his disciples what it means to be shepherd and sheep. Hearing his voice, they will follow. Trusting in him, they will be led to new pastures. Obeying him, they will be less prone to flight, even finding themselves abundantly sustained. With Jesus as the door, entrance into the faith is prepared. Do not flee from the quest, for the promise remains firm.

Call to Worship
LEADER: Jesus has said, I am the door; if any one enters by me, each one will be saved, and will go in and out and find pasture.

RESPONSE: Jesus came that those who believe in him may have life, and have it abundantly.

(Author's paraphrase)

Prayer of Praise and Adoration
Christ is the door by which we enter your new order, O God; he is the source of our comfort, and the anchor of our faith. Through him you have shown us the way unto the land of your promise, where peace is eternal and grace has no bounds. As we enter the courts of your sanctuary may we know you are with us, and give you all honor due your glorious name.

A Litany of Assurance
LEADER: When you do right and suffer for it patiently, you have God's approval.

RESPONSE: We are healed by Christ's wounds.

LEADER: For to this you have been called, that you should follow in Christ's steps.

RESPONSE: We are healed by Christ's wounds.

LEADER: He himself bore our sins in his body on the tree, that we might die to sin and live to righteousness.

RESPONSE: We are healed by Christ's wounds.

LEADER: For you were straying like sheep, but have now returned to the Shepherd and Guardian of your souls.

RESPONSE: We are healed by Christ's wounds.

LEADER: The Lord is my shepherd; I shall not be in want.

RESPONSE: We are healed by Christ's wounds.
LEADER: Though I walk through the valley of the shadow of death, I shall fear no evil; for God is with me.
RESPONSE: We are healed by Christ's wounds.

Prayer of Dedication

We hear the voice of Jesus the Shepherd, O God, and seek to follow his course for our lives. We bring our gifts now before you as results of our search. Accept them and use them so that others may join in the quest. Bring others to the gates of your promised land, and let them hear you calling them to come, enter in.

Prayer of Thanksgiving and Intercession

O God, you are the source of all life. All goodness and beauty flow from the depths of your being. You have caused the mountains to form and rise up; their valleys you clothe with blossoms, like a fine carpet woven with design. You give the birds freedom of flight; the fish search the depths of your oceans. The fields are fertile with the seeds of harvest. Cities teem with your people of many races and languages. You are the Great Designer who delights in creating. We give you thanks that you have placed us at the pinnacle of your plan. We are humbled by the honor you give and awed by your affirmation of us. May our service to others confirm our confession that you are God of our lives.

We pray for all who suffer this day from pains that are caused by others and those that are self-inflicted. Hear us, O God, as we intercede for sisters, brothers, and strangers who are wounded and long to be made whole. Bless doctors and nurses and all who support them as daily they minister to the sick and infirm. May clinics, hospitals, and places of convalescence be sources of hospice, giving hope to your people. May those who dispense drugs, and those who take them, do so in order to reduce disorders and disease. May those facing death retain dignity and be graced with the assurance that Christ lives in their midst. For those plagued by phobias that hinder their freedom, illumine their dark places by the light of your guidance. Fill the afflicted with the same Spirit that in Christ drove out demons. Since Jesus bore in his body on the tree all that grieves us, let us die to sin and live as those who are healed and forgiven.

FIFTH SUNDAY OF EASTER

Lectionary Readings for the Day
Ps. 31:1–8

Acts 7:55–60; I Peter 2:2–10; John 14:1–14

Seasonal Color:
White

As in God's house many rooms are to be found, so also in Christ's church many tasks are to be done. Jesus says that he is "the way, and the truth, and the life." Service among others is the way he portrays. The truth of the gospel is that God's people are free. The life that Christ offers removes the bondage to sin.

Call to Worship
LEADER: In you, O LORD, have I taken refuge;

RESPONSE: Incline your ear to me; make haste to deliver me.

LEADER: For the sake of your Name, lead me and guide me.

RESPONSE: Into your hands I commend my spirit, for you have redeemed me, O God of truth.

(BCP)

Prayer of Praise and Adoration
You are cause for rejoicing, O God, and the source of our gladness. You know what afflicts us; you can sense our distress. You remove whatever net will ensnare us; you give our feet firm places to stand. In Christ you have brought us deliverance. For all your mercies we praise your name and worship you now as our refuge and strength.

A Litany of Assurance
LEADER: Come to Christ, the living stone, chosen and precious in God's sight.

RESPONSE: We are a chosen race, a royal priesthood, a holy nation, God's own people.

LEADER: Like living stones be built yourselves into a spiritual house.

RESPONSE: We are a chosen race, a royal priesthood, a holy nation, God's own people.

LEADER: Offer spiritual sacrifices acceptable to God through Jesus Christ.

RESPONSE: We are a chosen race, a royal priesthood, a holy nation, God's own people.

LEADER: Declare the wonderful deeds of Christ who called you out of darkness into his marvelous light.

RESPONSE: We are a chosen race, a royal priesthood, a holy nation, God's own people.

LEADER: Once you were no people but now you are God's people; once you had not received mercy but now you have received mercy.

RESPONSE: We are a chosen race, a royal priesthood, a holy nation, God's own people.

Prayer of Dedication

As Jesus is the way, the truth, and the life, O God, may we in him find the source of our strength. As we carry gifts to you, empower our hands to lift others to Christ. As we offer our praise, place on our lips the good news of your love. As we hear your word spoken, lead us to new wisdom to impart the truth of the gospel: your people are free! Accept all that we do in the name of the Christ who makes all things new.

Prayer of Supplication

You open our eyes to your glory, O God; we see the Christ who stands by your side. He allows us to come into your presence and intercedes for us when we know not what to say. By his sacrifice he tore down the curtain that kept you at a distance because of the disobedience of your people. He showed us how much you love us and how you desire that we be kept near. In him you restore our confidence; you will not forsake us, or cast us away. So we approach you with assurance and boldness.

You have called us a chosen race, O God. Keep us mindful that you chose us for service and that it is your will we must heed. When we are arrogant, let the needs that surround us make us humble, so that your commandments may be obeyed. You have ordained us your royal priesthood, set apart for ministry. Help us to use the talents you give us, so that others may feed on the bread of life.

You have named us a holy nation. We plead your forgiveness when we forsake your redemptive society for our own patriotic zeal. Guide us as we take seriously our citizenship in your sacred order. Help us to exercise our electoral rights to the benefit of all those who remain powerless and without voice. You bestow a title upon us as we inherit in Christ the name of your people. Let us not look askance at the honor or take lightly the task it implies. The Spirit empowers us to respond with obedience, and by that guidance we seek to be faithful.

SIXTH SUNDAY OF EASTER

Lectionary Readings for the Day
Ps. 66:8–20
Acts 17:22–31; I Peter 3:13–22;   Seasonal Color:
John 14:15–21   White

With the promise of the Counselor comes an abiding sense of God's presence. Jesus has said that he will not leave us alone. His followers will know that as God is in him, so will he dwell in them. As the assurance is given, a task is assigned. Christ's commandments are at hand and they are to be kept. He is made manifest as his will is fulfilled.

Call to Worship
LEADER: Bless our God, you peoples; make the voice of [God's] praise to be heard.
RESPONSE: Blessed be God, who has not rejected my prayer, nor withheld [God's] love from me.
LEADER: Come and listen, all you who fear God, and I will tell you what [God] has done for me.
RESPONSE: Blessed be God, who has not rejected my prayer, nor withheld [God's] love from me.
LEADER: In truth God has heard me; [God] has attended to the voice of my prayer.
RESPONSE: Blessed be God, who has not rejected my prayer, nor withheld [God's] love from me.

(BCP)

Litany of Assurance
LEADER: Now who is there to harm you if you are zealous for what is right? Have no fear of them, nor be troubled.
RESPONSE: For Christ also died for sins once and for all, that he might bring us to God.
LEADER: Keep your conscience clear, so that those who revile your good behavior in Christ may be put to shame.
RESPONSE: For Christ also died for sins once and for all, that he might bring us to God.
LEADER: Baptism now saves you, as an appeal to God for a clear conscience, through the resurrection of Jesus Christ.
RESPONSE: For Christ also died for sins once and for all, that he might bring us to God.

LEADER: Christ has gone into heaven and is at the right hand of God, with angels, authorities, and powers subject to God.

RESPONSE: For Christ also died for sins once and for all, that he might bring us to God.

Prayer of Dedication

We come with assurance, O God, that you do not leave us alone. Your presence continues to guide us as we pursue the paths of discipleship. All that we have is a gift of your grace. As we offer gifts to you, accept them as signs of our commitment to Christ. May all that we do be in praise of your encompassing care.

Prayer of Thanksgiving and Supplication

O God, you neither need our praise nor want our burnt offerings. You have created the universe and all that therein dwells. All that we have or will become is an outpouring of your gracious care. You are God, with compassion and redemption flowing from the core of your being. You have sent us the Christ to set us aright. You allot the boundaries of our existence as his body the church. You determine the times for our ministry in his name. Apart from your mercy, we wander aimlessly through life. Yet you have looked with favor upon your people and for that we laud you with thanksgiving. In you we live, move, and have our being, and with that assurance we dare to give you all praise.

We look to your Spirit to fill us with counsel and guidance. Help us to learn what it means to be called your people. As the eight were saved through water in the covenant made with Noah, cleanse our conscience through the sacrifice of Jesus made once and for all. Fill us with zeal for the fulfillment of your commandments. Give us endurance and patience when the waters are troubled. May we tread bravely the way of the cross. As Christ has subjected all authorities and powers, rendering them mute upon hearing your word, attune us to your wisdom, to learn from the Scripture what you would have us do. You hide not yourself from us; our ignorance you do not overlook. Accept therefore our repentance through Jesus Christ, and fill us anew with the promise he lived and died to proclaim. As the Spirit pervades us, may we live in Christ to your eternal glory.

SEVENTH SUNDAY OF EASTER

Lectionary Readings for the Day
Ps. 68:1–10
Acts 1:6–14; I Peter 4:12–14; 5:6–11;   Seasonal Color:
John 17:1–11   White

Jesus prays to God with an outpouring of love on behalf of his people: that they will know God as the only true God; and that Christ may be glorified in God's presence as his words are made manifest among his disciples. May we strive to be one as Christ is at one with the only true God—that God's truth may be known.

Call to Worship
LEADER: The righteous are joyful, they exult before God, they are jubilant and shout for joy.
RESPONSE: Sing the praises of God, raise a psalm to his name.
(NEB)

Prayer of Praise and Adoration
We sing praises to you, O God; we raise a psalm in your honor. You clothe us in all goodness; we are draped in accordance with your design. As you have sent Jesus Christ to make your will known, you promise your Holy Spirit to guide us along your path. As your holiness fills our halls, hear us as we worship your name.

Litany of Assurance
LEADER: Rejoice in so far as you share Christ's sufferings, that you may be glad when Christ's glory is revealed.
RESPONSE: To God be the dominion for ever and ever.
LEADER: Humble yourselves under God's mighty hand, that in due time God may exalt you.
RESPONSE: To God be the dominion for ever and ever.
LEADER: Cast all your anxieties on God, for God cares about you.
RESPONSE: To God be the dominion for ever and ever.
LEADER: Be sober, be watchful. Your enemy the devil prowls around seeking some one to devour.
RESPONSE: To God be the dominion for ever and ever.

Prayer of Dedication

You pour out your love upon us, O God; you give us eternal life. As your mercy is made manifest in Jesus, may thanksgiving be shown by our gifts. Accept what we offer as signs of our humble gratitude for all that you do on our behalf. Make us useful servants of Christ in bringing your sons and daughters to a greater sense of your glory.

Prayer of Supplication

You put a song in our hearts, O God; our lips praise your name. The ordeals we face are nothing compared to the blessings you have in store for your people. If we are cast down, let it be because we seek to follow your way. You have sent Jesus Christ into the world to make known your will. He calls us and names us as your chosen people. Made right by his atoning sacrifice, we face boldly the tasks assigned us. Give us courage as we translate our confession into acts of reconciling love. Let us not be afraid to follow the example he set before us, but be encouraged by his intercession on our behalf. We submit our lives to you, yoked in harmony with what you command us to do. May our actions be an outburst of praise to your name, and our thoughts be in tune with the harmony you seek among the nations.

We yearn to be filled with the embracing presence of your Spirit. With our senses dulled by decisions that demand our attention we need to be focused on what you want us to do. Give us some discipline to determine your desire, and equip us to fulfill your demands. Our hands droop at times when they should reach out to support others, and knees become weak when our feet seek your straight path. Jar us out of our listless ways and enliven us with your quickening power. When we are shortsighted or misuse your grace, chasten our choices by your judgment, and replace our schemes with your design for our lives. Deliver us from the undue need to control our own destiny, and from anxiety when our fate is uncertain. Prepare us to be responsive to the counsel of your Spirit, and thereby be led to new ventures of faith. May we who are your flock find dwelling in your goodness, O God, and, secure in your love, find that boldness to serve others.

beyond the farthest

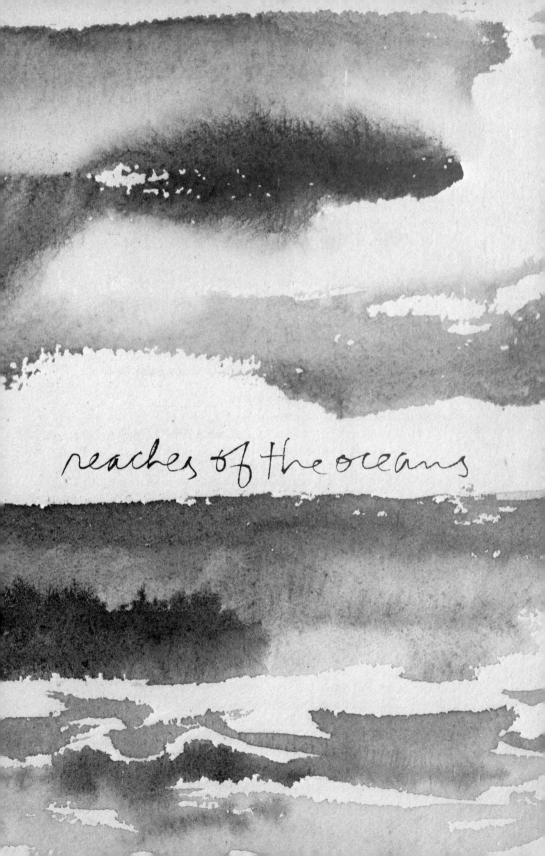

reaches of the oceans

THE DAY OF PENTECOST

Lectionary Readings for the Day
Ps. 104:24–34

Acts 2:1–21; I Cor. 12:3b–13; John 7:37–39

Seasonal Color:
Red

Remember your baptism! Those are appropriate words for this day. Believers in Christ are cleansed with living water. The Spirit bestows the truth of God's grace. The community, called the church, surrounds the baptized, as one is engrafted into the body of Christ. Pentecost is the day of one's birth into God's Kingdom. Come, let us celebrate!

Call to Worship
LEADER: I will sing to the LORD as long as I live, all my life I will sing psalms to my God.

RESPONSE: May my meditation please the LORD, as I show my joy in him!

LEADER: Bless the LORD, my soul. O praise the LORD.

(NEB)

Prayer of Praise and Adoration
We sing psalms of praise, O God; we gather in praise of your name. You send your Spirit into our midst filling us with the promise of new life. We are aglow with the light that Christ shines on the new day, dispelling the darkness of the night that has passed. Be among us to gather our words of adoration and be in us as we seek to obey your will.

Prayer of Confession
UNISON: With new life all about us, O God, we still cling to old ways. In spite of your promises we seek self-assurance. You send the Holy Spirit to enliven our existence. The darkness of doubt dispels the new light the Spirit brings. We are afraid to admit what it might mean if we surrendered our selves. So we continue to pursue our flights of fancy, and pretend that we can go it alone.

Assurance of Pardon
LEADER: God has mercy upon us and hears our confession. In Christ we have the assurance that we dwell not alone. All who approach God with a desire for wholeness will be filled with living waters, which the Spirit gives. Be refreshed in your quest

to do what is faithful, and be alive with the promise of God's guidance and care.

Prayer of Dedication

With many voices we praise you, O God; in different ways we serve you. Take our diversity and mold it into a common theme of thanksgiving. Weave these gifts that we bring into a whole cloth of service that will blanket the world with your love as we announce with one accord your truth which sets us free.

Prayer of Thanksgiving

With many voices we give you thanks, O God. By your Spirit blend our utterances into a symphony of praise worthy of your name. You have stretched out the heavens and set the earth on its course. You have raised up the mountains; the valleys you laid low. The trees you cause to rise toward the sun; their branches provide haven for birds. You bring the rain in its season to water the earth. You prepare the fields for the harvest. Silos are filled with the yield you occasion, and our tables are spread with your bounty. You place the moon over us by night, the sun above us to warm our day. The tides ebb and flow in response to your bidding, and the winds blow as you direct them. You are God, who is above us and below us, before us and behind us, watching over us and caring for us, directing the way we shall go.

We give you thanks for the Holy Spirit, who guides, giving us gifts by which to respond to your will. Some among us utter wisdom and knowledge; we give you thanks for their minds. May they be led to further their thinking, that we may become more enlightened with increasing truth. Some in our midst have gifts of healing; we give you thanks for their compassion and patience. In their search to ease the suffering of others, may they help overcome the causes of pain. Some work with their hands or fashion fine art; we give you thanks for their imagination and skill. May their creations be tributes that honor your name, and reminders to us that we serve you alone. There are some with good business sense, others with talents they volunteer; we give you thanks for their discipline and service. Help us to learn from them how to use our time wisely, to apportion our talents so that others rejoice. You amaze us, O God, with the breadth of your love. You continue to fill us with the breath of your Spirit. For all your mercies we give you thanks.

TRINITY SUNDAY

Lectionary Readings for the Day

Ps. 33:1–12; Deut. 4:32–40

II Cor. 13:5–14; Matt. 28:16–20

Seasonal Color:
White

The disciples went to Galilee, and there met the risen Christ on the mountain. We are told that they worshiped him, even though some doubted. Christ spoke with authority and gave them a task. Since then, people have ventured into all nations, teaching what Jesus commanded. As people continue to labor in the shadow of Christ's cross, others are enabled to delight in the radiance of its glory.

Call to Worship

LEADER: Rejoice in the LORD, you righteous; it is good for the just to sing praises.

RESPONSE: For the word of the LORD is right, and all [of God's] works are sure.

LEADER: Let all the earth fear the LORD; let all who dwell in the world stand in awe of [God].

RESPONSE: Happy is the nation whose God is the LORD! happy the people [God] has chosen to be [God's] own!

(BCP)

Prayer of Praise and Adoration

We do indeed stand in awe of you, O God. We rejoice that you have chosen us to be your own. By your word the heavens were made; your loving kindness fills the whole earth. By the bounty of your mercy we have been born to new life. Hear now what fanfare we give you as our voices are lifted in praise of your name.

Prayer of Confession

UNISON: O God, when we are put to the test we do not quickly respond. If called upon to decide, we lack the courage of faith. Confessing commitment, we confuse your will with our own. Seeking security, we turn to devices that we control. Your voice comes from heaven to chasten and discipline. Your commandments Jesus proclaimed as the course we should take. Forgive us when we deviate from the truth you deliver, and increase our trust in you.

Assurance of Pardon

LEADER: As Jesus met his disciples on the mountain, he is with us today, even to the close of the age. With authority he commissions us to service; with redeeming love he sets us aright when we fall. All who humbly approach him seeking forgiveness for their sins can live with assurance, since Christ died for us all.

Prayer of Dedication

You call us to labor, O God, and to be about the tasks you design. You equip us to serve you, and care for all our needs. The gifts that we offer are but a portion of the treasures you heap on us. May the work that we do be worthy of your name. Take what we bring and all that we are and fashion our responses to meet your standards for faith.

Prayer of Thanksgiving and Petition

O God of deliverance, you brought forth a nation from bondage. You spoke out of the midst of the fire, delivering commandments that gave freedom to your people. With your mighty hand you encompassed them, with an outstretched arm you enfolded them. We give you thanks for these foremothers and forefathers who are our family in faith.

You sent your Son Jesus to redeem us from sin. He was tempted and suffered, yet remained obedient even unto death. The grave could not hold him, for he stands by your side. We give you thanks that he atones for our sins and intercedes on our behalf. As he calls us into his household, help us to obey him through the guidance of your Spirit. Inflame us with zeal for devotion to your way. Order our thinking and our acting, so that our total behavior accords with what you command.

We pray for those who serve Christ's household in other lands. We give you thanks for their courage, which remains a badge of their boldness. We hold high their vision of wholeness, as they go about teaching and healing your people. They have remembered their baptism, and thereby revealed the gifts of your new order. When we despair of our dwindling vitality, inspire us by their talk of renewal. If we are prone to be parochial, hold them as a testimony to your universal love. As your disciples went to Galilee, and there met Christ on the mountain, let your world be our arena, and that same Christ our source of strength. As your people everywhere labor in the shadow of Christ's cross, may we bathe in the radiance of your unending glory.

SECOND SUNDAY AFTER PENTECOST

Lectionary Readings for the Day

Ps. 33:12–22; Gen. 12:1–9   Seasonal Color:
Rom. 3:21–28; Matt. 7:21–29   Green

A steadfast foundation can make a great difference. When battered by the elements, the structure built thereon will endure. Jesus reminds his hearers how his words provide such stability. Yet words alone do not suffice. Just as a foundation lacks shape without further framework, words without actions are less than complete. The support has been given to proceed with constructing one's faith.

Call to Worship

LEADER: Our soul waits for the LORD; [God] is our help and our shield.

RESPONSE: Let your loving-kindness, O [God,] be upon us, as we have put our trust in you.

(BCP)

Prayer of Praise and Adoration

Your eye is upon us, O God; you see our going out and our coming in. You know when we gather in praise of your name. You are aware of our needs, how our souls yearn for peace. You are compassionate and tender, embracing us with your love. Hear us in our whispering and listen to our shouting as we herald your honor this day.

Prayer of Confession

UNISON: O God, have mercy upon us as you hear our confession. We are prone to do work to earn your favor and grace. You have taught us that Jesus is the source of salvation, yet we unceasingly strive to save our own souls. Time becomes an encumbrance when there is so much to do. We scarcely have strength to accomplish demands. Teach us again of your acceptance in Jesus, and release us from bondage to our own striving for perfection.

Assurance of Pardon

LEADER: As Paul reminds us, "since all have sinned and fall short of the glory of God, they are justified by God's grace as a gift, through the redemption which is in Christ Jesus." In the name of Jesus Christ we are justified by faith.

Prayer of Dedication

We know, O God, that words without actions are less than complete. As we confess Jesus as our Savior, we commit our lives to your care. Enable us to serve you with boldness, enlivened by the promise of your unending presence. Accept the gifts that we offer as signs of our devotion. May they announce to your people that your will shall be done.

Prayer of Thanksgiving and Supplication

O God of the living word, hear our prayer. By your word Sarah, Abraham, and Lot left their homeland. Through your grace they became a great nation. They obeyed your decree and called on your name. We give thanks that they believed in your promise as they journeyed with faith.

With your word you established the household of Christ. You secured its foundation through the gift of your Son. You set forth the commandments of love and obedience. We give thanks that by disclosing your will, you govern your people, and teach us how to behave.

Your word corrects us and gives us hope. Your promises do not fail us, but allow us to live by grace. As Jesus became the word ever present, and abides with us still to deliver us blameless, we thank you for your mercy, and commit ourselves anew to walk in faith.

We pray for discernment to understand what you say. Amid the rabble of voices that beckon us to listen, keep us attuned to that still, small voice. When pressures beset us, and we are forced to make choices, encourage us as we accept your will for our lives. Amid sensors, computers, condensers, and chips we are a people of technology who communicate with skill. May that efficiency be as effective in understanding your will.

We pray for enthusiasm as we lead others to Christ. We are a people who proclaim him our Savior and Friend. May how we live convince others of the changes he wrought, as he went about listening to those who had needs. When the rains fall, and the winds blow, let our faith be as a rock upon which others can stand. As we hear anew the words that Christ spoke, let us give strength to the weak, courage to the fainthearted, comfort to the fearful, and nourishment to the hungry. So dwell within us that what we say and do declares your love to be higher than the heavens and your faithfulness to extend to the farthest reaches of the skies.

THIRD SUNDAY AFTER PENTECOST

Lectionary Readings for the Day
Ps. 13; Gen. 22:1–18

Rom. 4:13–18; Matt. 9:9–13

Seasonal Color:

Green

Those at table with Jesus were judged by others as unworthy of such honor. Mercy is often misunderstood in this way. Those who think they deserve it are seldom receptive to others being included. The ones invited in spite of their faults often bring little to commend such distinction. Mercy provides a place at the table, where those who hunger for righteousness may be fed.

Call to Worship
LEADER: I put my trust in your mercy; [O God,] my heart is joyful because of your saving help.

RESPONSE: I will sing to the LORD, for [God] has dealt with me richly; I will praise the Name of [God] Most High.
(BCP)

Prayer of Praise and Adoration
It is right to give you praise and honor, O God, for your love endures forever. As your people gather to give your name glory, they shall come from east and west, from north and south. We are assembled together as those redeemed by your Son; may what we say be a blessing worthy of your hearing, and what we do a service befitting your glory.

Prayer of Confession
UNISON: O God, you spread your table before us and invite us to dine. We judge some as unworthy to partake of your feast. You call us to faith in the Lord Jesus Christ. We close the doors of your household to those we deem unfit to come in. You desire mercy, not sacrifice, as a response to your grace. We expect others to be thankful that we accept them at all. Forgive us our arrogance in response to your love. Make us mindful of those whom you also hold dear.

Assurance of Pardon
LEADER: Jesus has said: "Those who are well have no need of a physician, but those who are sick. Go and learn what this means, 'I desire mercy, and not sacrifice.' For I came not to call the righteous, but sinners." If we are honest and confess our sins

before God, we inherit the righteousness of faith revealed in Jesus Christ.

Prayer of Dedication

O God, you crown us with distinction and honor. You lavish us with gifts in abundance. You spread your mercy before us as a host preparing a banquet. What we offer, you have already given to us. What we do with our hands is a gift of the life you breathe into us. We give you but your own, a legacy of your love and concern.

Prayer of Thanksgiving

Nations are formed according to your design, O God. People are gathered to suit your purpose. You call us together and give us our names; you set us apart and fix our boundaries. You have peopled the world with many colors and features: many languages are spoken and different customs are observed. You are like one who weaves a rich tapestry with fine cloth, where each thread is important to the blend you desire. We rejoice in the splendor of the mix you have created, and offer our thanksgiving for the composite you intend us to be.

We give you thanks for the vision that those of faith have brought to this land. For the Native Americans who were here long before. They taught us to live at peace with your earth. Remind us by their presence how dependent we are on your created order. We thank you for those who left homelands and ventured across seas. They came with dreams of new beginnings and built a country rich in opportunity. May the diversity of our ethnic origins serve as a composite that brings wholeness and health. We thank you for men and women of color, those who came shackled and bound. They have given us a legacy of hope and determination. Let them not flag in their zeal for a society free of bigotry and hate. We give you thanks for the freedoms we enjoy: For the freedom of religion; all praise be unto you. For the freedom of the press; help our search for the truth to accord with your will. For the freedom from want; serving Christ, we commit ourselves to overcome injustice and greed. For the freedom to assemble; may our gatherings bring peace, not discord.

Once nations are formed they also need to mature. O God, you are our strength and deliverance. For your mercy, patience, comfort, and grace, we give you thanks and applaud your design.

Lectionary Readings for the Day

Ps. 46; Gen. 25:19–34

Rom. 5:6–11; Matt. 9:35 to 10:8

Seasonal Color:

Green

Jesus had compassion on the helpless and infirm. The disciples were sent to heal and to cleanse. Wherever they went, the Kingdom of Heaven was proclaimed in their midst. The harvest is still plentiful, and laborers continue to be in demand. There are the sick for whom health care is needed. The hungry still wait to be fed. Go forth to your fields of labor.

Call to Worship

LEADER: Let be then: learn that I am God, high over the nations, high above earth.

RESPONSE: God is our shelter and our refuge, a timely help in trouble.

(NEB)

Prayer of Praise and Adoration

O God, you shelter your people amid their distress; you provide them a haven of security and rest. You bring comfort to those with affliction, and hear the pleas of the persecuted. You cause your mercy to flow like living water; your benevolence stretches to the ends of the earth. We come in praise of all your goodness and lift our voices with thanks for your care.

Prayer of Confession

UNISON: O God, like Jacob with Esau we struggle for rights. We grapple with others to give us our due. Contentment comes slowly when we don't get our fair share. We confess our impatience when others misuse us. We confess our dislike for those who deny us. Forgive our distrust that you will care for our needs. Help us to strive for equal justice for all.

Assurance of Pardon

LEADER: Hear what Paul writes: "While we were still weak, at the right time Christ died for the ungodly. . . . If while we were enemies we were reconciled to God by the death of God's Son, much more, now that we are reconciled, shall we be saved by Christ's life." We may rejoice in God through Jesus Christ, through whom we receive reconciliation.

Prayer of Dedication

You urge us to travel lightly and proclaim your peace. Relieve us of whatever hinders our mission, and give to us sustenance for the journey. The gifts we offer are symbols of our commitment; by whatever peace we foster, help us to heal antagonisms that divide your people; and may our actions provide hospitality even in the midst of hostility.

Prayer of Thanksgiving and Petition

O God of Rebekah and Isaac, God of birth who conceives the nations, you have brought forth a people as a mother delivers a child. You have suckled them with the milk of kindness, holding them close and away from harm's door. You have nurtured them with your wisdom, while cleansing them at the font of living waters. You have chastised them and cajoled them when their obedience has waned. Your judgment has not been wanting when they strayed from your ways. You have caused Christ to come forth, conceived by your Spirit of reconciling love. He grew up with stature in accordance with your will. Submissive to your commandments, he was vulnerable to the needs of others. He stooped to lift the weak out of their depths of despair. His authority you gave to him, his destiny you designed, his death you determined on behalf of us all. We live with hope because of your care. We inherit the promise of new life because of your compassion.

With such a witness of your sustaining indulgence before us, help us to show sympathy to others. Send us forth to labor in the name of Christ Jesus. Equip us with tongues to proclaim to them your word. Give us keen minds to detect the causes of injustice and oppression. Make us resourceful in devising means to expose and eliminate persecution. Help us to stand in rapport with the downtrodden, as we accompany them through the gates of your redeemed society.

We pray for the sick and those shut in for whatever reason. Give cheer to our voices as we greet them in the name of Christ Jesus. May our arms embrace them with your encompassing care. Open our hearts to their plight, as with our hands we seek to lift them to a sense of their dignity. As we are able to lead them to wholeness we laud your benevolent support for all your children, and thank you for kindness by which you hear this our prayer.

FIFTH SUNDAY AFTER PENTECOST

Lectionary Readings for the Day

Ps. 91:1–10; Gen. 28:10–17   Seasonal Color:

Rom. 5:12–19; Matt. 10:24–33   Green

There need be no fear among those called God's people, since there is nothing still hidden from God. What was covered is now revealed; what was secret is made known, and the message earlier whispered is now shouted. Two sparrows are worth merely a penny, yet God is aware of their fate. How much more will God know of your needs, when even the hairs of your head are numbered?

Call to Worship

LEADER: You who dwell in the shelter of the Most High, who abide in the shadow of the Almighty, will say,

RESPONSE: My refuge and my fortress; my God, in whom I trust.

Prayer of Praise and Adoration

You are indeed our refuge and our fortress, O God, giving us a haven against our fears and security in the face of our enemies. You become weak so that we can be strong; Christ suffers judgment so that we can be blessed. You stoop to hear our plaintive cries and rise up to proclaim your word to us. We bow down in submission to what you want us to do; we stand in praise of your name.

Prayer of Confession

UNISON: O God, in Christ Jesus, have mercy upon us. We are not quick to proclaim Christ as our savior. We have our own desires that demand our devotion. Other people have power over us that we dare not deny. We sometimes confuse Christ's will and our own. At times it is awkward to confess him the source of new life. With compassion he suffers, aware of our plight. O God, hear our confession, and through Christ keep us upright.

Assurance of Pardon

LEADER: Paul writes that "if, because of one's trespass, death reigned . . . , much more will those who receive the abundance of grace and the free gift of righteousness reign in life through

. . . Jesus Christ." We may live anew, with the assurance of Jesus Christ who reigns in us.

Prayer of Dedication

O God, we have been led to acknowledge Christ Jesus as the source of new life. With Jacob we have a vision of your heaven before us. As you have called us to be your people, we come before you offering our gifts. Use them to spread your message from east to west and from south to north. Lead our descendants to proclaim you God of their lives.

Prayer of Thanksgiving and Petition

You open the gates of heaven, O God, and we catch sight of your eternal order. Your way of righteousness and peace is made known in Jesus, who announces the dawn of a new age. You invite us as citizens of your holy city, where justice and order prevail. Your commandments become our guide and direction in how to discern your will. Jesus has shown us what it means to obey; he has made what was hidden now known. As the light he illumines our way, and makes common what once we feared. We thank you that as we face that which lies ahead, we can approach you with assurance that our past is forgiven. You know of our needs before we announce them; by your grace we greet the new day. As we continue to dwell in your mercy, we thank you for that sustaining presence. Through the guidance of the Holy Spirit as our counselor, we seek to fulfill what you expect us to be.

We pray for our nation and the role we perform as citizens. Help us to take responsibility for our actions so that others become able to respond. Keep us from ignoring those who are in need, either because we are greedy or we think them inferior. Guide us to measure our own generosity by the magnitude of your benevolence. When we read of issues that confront us, keep us from complacency and apathy. May we not abrogate our inherent right to speak, out of fear that our voices will go unheard. Help us to assist those who have been elected to office, those we have entrusted to govern. Participating with them in the process, help us to provide them with the benefit of our thoughts. We pray for the leaders of our country and other nations as well. Give to them a sense of humility amid the power they exercise. May they foster more humane ways of making decisions than with threats and the instruments of war. Endow within them respect for each other, so that all your people can dwell in the hope that the peace you ordain does in fact prevail.

SIXTH SUNDAY AFTER PENTECOST

Lectionary Readings for the Day
Ps. 17:1–7, 15; Gen. 32:22–32

Rom. 6:3–11; Matt. 10:34–42

Seasonal Color:

Green

A cross is heavy and burdensome to carry. It takes most of the energy that one can muster. It limits peripheral vision, keeping one's eyes fixed straight on the road. To lay it down in order to rest creates problems; it will need to be lifted again. To set it aside and ignore it would be easiest. But then Christ wasn't given that option. To follow means bearing a cross.

Call to Worship
LEADER: Yahweh, hear the plea of virtue, listen to my appeal, lend an ear to my prayer, my lips free from dishonesty.

RESPONSE: I have treasured the words from your lips, walking deliberately in your footsteps, so that my feet do not slip.

LEADER: I invoke you, God, and you answer me; turn your ear to me, hear what I say, display your marvellous kindness, saviour of fugitives!

RESPONSE: For me the reward of virtue is to see your face, and, on waking, to gaze my fill on your likeness.

(JB)

Prayer of Praise and Adoration
O God, you hear our pleas and listen to our appeals. You watch over our nights and fill our days with your presence. You cause our feet to stand on firm places and give our eyes visions of your kindness and mercy. Hear us now as we gather to praise and adore you. Speak to us that we may learn of your ways.

A Litany of Confession
LEADER: Do you not know that all of us who have been baptized into Christ Jesus were baptized into his death?

RESPONSE: Forgive, O God, our unwillingness to accept your truth.

LEADER: As Christ was raised from the dead by the glory of God, we too might walk in newness of life.

RESPONSE: Forgive, O God, our stubbornness to follow.

LEADER: We know that our old self was crucified so that we might no longer be enslaved to sin.

RESPONSE: Forgive us, O God, when we yield to temptation.

LEADER: If we have died with Christ, we believe that we shall also live with him.

RESPONSE: Forgive us, O God, when we lack courage and conviction.

LEADER: So you also must consider yourselves dead to sin and alive to God in Christ Jesus.

RESPONSE: Have mercy upon us, O God, and help us to come alive in Christ.

Prayer of Dedication

"In the cross of Christ I glory, towering o'er the wrecks of time; all the light of sacred story gathers round its head sublime." As we glory in the cross of Christ, O God, so we also seek to serve the cause for which he died. Accept the gifts placed before you as symbols of our commitment. May the light of your sacred story shine forth for all to see.

Prayer of Thanksgiving

O God, when you wrestled with Jacob, you marked him, named him, and called him your own. You called forth a people and with your oath you promised that they would endure. You gave them the law, and you went before them by night and by day. We give you thanks for Jacob, Leah, and Rachel, and their descendants.

We give you thanks for Christ Jesus, whose name we now bear through baptism. He went about teaching what it means to obey. He fulfilled your law as he served all those in need. By his death he atoned for the sins of your people. He interceded for all as he was hung on a cross. But death could not keep him, and he lives now in our midst.

We give you thanks for the Holy Spirit, who guides us today. The Spirit serves as assurance that you do not leave us alone. The Spirit instills in us zeal, so that we perform tasks in accord with your will. By the Spirit we are led to people in want; confronted by thorny issues and prodded to enlarge our horizons.

We give you thanks for the Scripture that bears witness to your presence. The words leap from the pages and challenge our timid ways. Keep us mindful, O God, of those who have gone before us and of the history in which we stand.

SEVENTH SUNDAY AFTER PENTECOST

Lectionary Readings for the Day
Ps. 124; Ex. 1:6–14, 22 to 2:10   Seasonal Color:
Rom. 7:14–25a; Matt. 11:25–30   Green

Whereas each person alone must bear a cross, a yoke is worn jointly. When Christ commands the one, at the same time he promises the other. Our labor is faithfully to follow Christ's way. The hope is his word that he will teach us the path. Our rest is the assurance that he knows of our burdens. The task is to join him in the venture called faith.

Call to Worship
LEADER: Our help is in the name of the LORD, who made heaven and earth.
RESPONSE: Thanks be to God through Jesus Christ our Lord!
LEADER: Let us worship God.

Prayer of Praise and Adoration
You are our guardian and our shield, O God, our protector who keeps us from falling. You surround us with righteousness that wards off evil forces; in Christ is assurance to withstand ways that may tempt us. You shower us with your mercy that cleanses wrongdoing. You temper your judgment with compassion. We stand in adoration and in praise of your name.

Litany of Confession
LEADER: There is therefore now no condemnation for those who are in Christ Jesus.
RESPONSE: I do not understand my own actions. For I do not do what I want, but I do the very thing I hate.
LEADER: There is therefore now no condemnation for those who are in Christ Jesus.
RESPONSE: So then it is no longer I that do it, but sin which dwells within me.
LEADER: There is therefore now no condemnation for those who are in Christ Jesus.
RESPONSE: I can will what is right, but I cannot do it.
LEADER: There is therefore now no condemnation for those who are in Christ Jesus.
RESPONSE: Miserable creature that I am! Who is there to deliver this body of death?

LEADER: God alone, through Jesus Christ our Lord!
RESPONSE: Thanks be to God!

Prayer of Dedication

O God, as we are in ministry with sisters and brothers through-out the world, collectively and individually we seek obediently to answer Christ's call. Use the gifts that we offer to enhance our work to your glory. Let them provide guidance for the venture called faith. Link us as partners and unite us to serve you wher-ever we dwell.

Prayer of Thanksgiving and Supplication

O God of judgment and liberation, we give you thanks for delivering your people from the perils that confront them. You gave Moses a haven along the banks of the Nile. You caused him to be nurtured by his mother and to grow in your favor. You protected a nation from the anger of its enemies. When hosts of armies rose up against them, threatening to engulf them like a flood of raging waters, you stilled the tempest, and your people escaped into safety. You sent Jesus Christ to liberate them from bondage. At war with themselves they have been redeemed by your grace. Once and for all you have in Christ offered freedom from sin. We live as a testimony to your love and stand with confidence in the face of your judgment.

Your mercy continues to shield us as we seek faithfully to follow your will. Save us from ourselves when we do foolish things. We pray, "Lead us not into temptation," and we ask that you will hear us. Give us wisdom and surround us with guidance as we act out Christ's call. As foes taunt us or defame our good name, help us find in your love strength to endure. Give us courage to do battle on behalf of the oppressed. May our measure of conviction make us bold to suffer for their sakes. Armed with the breastplate of righteousness, let us never lose heart, as we wage war against enemies of your desire for peace.

You preserve us and nurture us and keep us from falling. Through our Savior Christ Jesus our lives are secure. As you led your people through peril, continue to deliver us from the evil that surrounds us. As you sent Christ into the world for our sakes, may we courageously serve in his name, secure in the promise that you name us your own.

EIGHTH SUNDAY AFTER PENTECOST

Lectionary Readings for the Day
Ps. 69:6–15; Ex. 2:11–22

Rom. 8:9–17; Matt. 13:1–9, 18–23

Seasonal Color:
Green

When seeds are sown along various routes, the results can be precisely predicted. If no thought is given to their nourishment, they will be snatched and taken away. If they are fed for a time, then forgotten, their life will be fleeting at best. When their care is sporadic, other growth will get in their way. It is best that they be tended with care; then their growth and their yield will be great.

Call to Worship
LEADER: I lift up this prayer to thee, O LORD: accept me now in thy great love.

RESPONSE: Answer me with thy sure deliverance, O God.

(NEB)

Prayer of Praise and Adoration
Our prayers are lifted to you, O God; you deliver your people during times of distress. You show sorrow for those who are afflicted; you rejoice with those who abound with happiness. As you caused Christ Jesus to be raised from the dead, we awaken now to your promise of new life. Your Spirit fills us with your presence as we praise you our God and comforter evermore.

Litany of Assurance
LEADER: You are not in the flesh, you are in the Spirit, if the Spirit of God really dwells in you.

RESPONSE: For all who are led by the Spirit of God are the children of God.

LEADER: If the Spirit of God dwells in you, God who raised Christ Jesus from the dead will give life to your mortal bodies.

RESPONSE: For all who are led by the Spirit of God are the children of God.

LEADER: If by the Spirit you put to death the deeds of the body you will live.

RESPONSE: For all who are led by the Spirit of God are the children of God.

LEADER: We are God's heirs, and heirs with Christ, provided we share his suffering now in order to share his splendor hereafter.

RESPONSE: For all who are led by the Spirit of God are the children of God.

Prayer of Dedication

As Moses named Gershom, so you call us sojourners. Send us, O Christ, into the world to sow your seeds of righteousness and peace. We offer ourselves to your service with the prayer that we become receptive to your command. Nourish us with the gift of your Spirit that we may grow more pleasing in your sight. We pray that the fruit of our faith shall lead others to you.

Prayer of Thanksgiving and Supplication

O God our refuge and strength, as you deliver your people from the oppressor, you accompany them on their journeys. You give them bread to sustain them and the fruit of the vine to make glad their hearts. You cause the earth to nourish the seeds, the wheat and the corn to flower and yield grain in abundance. The comb fills with honey from nectar you have hidden in the blossoms; the pine bears its cones to feed your friends in the forest. You are God of all living things; you designed the creation with an eye for beauty. We partake of your splendor, and give thanks for your grandeur. Grant us humility as we offer our prayer.

We are your sojourners in our quest to be faithful. Help us to be more receptive to the seeds of your love. As your word is delivered, there are those who distort it and purge it of meaning. They render it innocuous with impact impaired. Give us the insight to discern your message, and the courage to confess trust in your truth. At times our hearts are hardened by the trials that confront us. Tribulation tempts us to turn away from you. We build idols and monuments to support our security; they are shorn of your wisdom and do not weather the storm. Give us the hindsight to learn from past deeds, and the foresight to depend on your word.

At times we choke on consumption of society's goods. We take a fancy to gadgets and entrust our well-being to them. Surrounded by such objects, we yet hunger for stability. Temper our desires with your compassion, and help us to surrender ourselves to your protective care. May our understanding and obedience be in accordance with what you desire, so that in our quest to be faithful the yield of our labor may be pleasing in your sight.

NINTH SUNDAY AFTER PENTECOST

Lectionary Readings for the Day
Ps. 103:1–13; Ex. 3:1–12　　　　　　　　　Seasonal Color:
Rom. 8:18–25; Matt. 13:24–30, 36–43　　　　　　　　　Green

The wheat and the seeds represent the way of God's Kingdom in the midst of the world. False doctrine and misplaced allegiance exist alongside God's truth and God's will. When the harvest occurs there will be judgment. What bears good fruit will be gathered and stored. The useless will be cast aside. Jesus reminds those who hear to take note.

Call to Worship
LEADER:　Bless the LORD, O my soul, and all that is within me, bless [God's] holy Name.
RESPONSE:　Bless the LORD, O my soul, and forget not all [God's] benefits.
LEADER:　The LORD is full of compassion and mercy, slow to anger and of great kindness.
RESPONSE:　For as the heavens are high above the earth, so is [God's] mercy great upon those who fear [God].
(BCP)

Prayer of Praise and Adoration
O God, we gather to bless you for bountiful mercy, for the compassion and care you extend to us. You surround us with a mantle that protects us from danger; our breastplate is your righteousness fulfilled in Christ Jesus. You are our shield and defender, our hope and our comfort. We give you all praise as we assemble in Christ's name.

Prayer of Confession
UNISON: We confess, O God, that our lives are a mixture of weeds and good seeds. The weeds choke us and limit our will to respond. The good seeds we admire and want to nourish. When the harvest comes, we know that the good will be kept and all else will be judged unfit for your reign. Christ have mercy upon us as we learn of your will. Give us guidance and determination as we obey your command. Forgive our misplaced allegiance when we settle for weeds. May we broadcast the landscape with the good seed of your word.

Assurance of Pardon

LEADER: Paul writes of our assurance when he says: "We know that the whole creation has been groaning in travail together until now; and not only the creation, but we ourselves, who have the first fruits of the Spirit, groan inwardly as we wait for adoption as children, the redemption of our bodies. For in this hope we are saved."

Prayer of Dedication

As the wheat is gathered into the barns, O God, so the fruits of our labors are brought into your house. Through the purging fire of your judgment, render our gifts acceptable in your sight. Set them aside as worthy, so that others may be nourished by Jesus Christ, the bread of life.

Prayer of Thanksgiving

You are God of Abraham and Sarah, Isaac and Rebekah, Jacob, Leah and Rachel, Joseph and Asenath, Moses and Zipporah. From them has come a mighty people you have chosen to call your own. You have spoken through your prophets; your priests have taught your people how to worship your name. With wisdom, scribes have delivered your word; with poetry, writers have penned praise in your honor. Nations have been brought to submission in the face of your judgment. History has recorded testimony of your mercy that has withstood the ages. What are we compared to your grandeur and grace?

Yet, in love you sent us your Son Jesus Christ. He walked among your people and taught them your will. He enlightened his followers to the sense of your commandments. He stooped to hear the plight of the stranger and cast out demons from those who were oppressed. He suffered the shame of the cross for the sins of all your people, and even now pulls us from the pit of our own disgrace and shame. The grave cannot contain your righteous deliverance; he lives as our mediator and guide.

We give you thanks, O God, for this perspective on your providence. It sheds light on the sufferings that we endure in our time. You surround us with hope as we seek to be faithful; you give a glimpse of your glory as we groan in travail. Make us mindful of all who are part of the household of God. Let the legacy that they bequeath be a source of inspiration as with confidence we interpret your will for our time.

TENTH SUNDAY AFTER PENTECOST

Lectionary Readings for the Day

Ps. 105:1–11; Ex. 3:13–20
Rom. 8:26–30; Matt. 13:44–52

Seasonal Color:
Green

The Kingdom of Heaven is like a treasure of great value. Much will be sacrificed in order to possess it. Its worth is so obvious that its presence is protected. In order to retain its purity the superfluous is cast aside. Christ died that all may have life. God sends the Spirit so that God's truth may be known. When Jesus calls us to discipleship he bids us to forsake former ways.

Call to Worship

LEADER: Give thanks to the LORD and call upon [God's] Name; make known [God's] deeds among the peoples.
RESPONSE: Sing to [God,] sing praises to [God], and speak of all [God's] marvelous works.
LEADER: Glory in [God's] holy Name; let the hearts of those who seek the LORD rejoice.
RESPONSE: Search for the LORD and continually seek [God's] face.
(BCP)

Prayer of Praise and Adoration

Your face, O God, we seek, as we call on your name. You hear us when we implore your mercy, and grant us your grace that fills us with joy. We are your people, the heirs of your promise. We enter Christ's household in response to his call. Fill us now with your Spirit. Form us and mold us as we extol you with praise.

Prayer of Confession

UNISON: O God, have mercy upon us as we make our confession. We question your judgment when your will conflicts with our own. We are reluctant to follow the course you prescribe. Our patience grows thin when you intrude in life's journey, causing us to veer from the path we pursue. We seek to be faithful and obey your directions, but our own desires delay us in fulfilling your will. Have mercy upon us and deliver us from self-deception.

Assurance of Pardon

LEADER: Paul assures us that the Spirit helps us in our weakness, and intercedes for us according to God's will. In Jesus Christ, God calls us, and conforms us to Christ, so that in him we receive the promise of new life. As we dwell in the Spirit let us also rest assured in the promise.

Prayer of Dedication

Treasures lose their luster, and riches are easily spent, but your kingdom endures forever. We approach you, O God, trusting your will for our lives. You give us assurance of your abiding presence. You provide us with confidence as we follow Christ's call. Accept now the gifts that we offer, so that your truth may be known throughout the land.

Prayer of Thanksgiving and Supplication

We know you as God who is and shall be, one who with might performs wonders and with graciousness bestows manifold blessings. You speak and the heavens thunder with the sound of your voice. You stretch forth your hand and even the sparrows find safe lodging. In Christ Jesus you chose to walk among your people, revealing in him your marvelous love. As your Holy Spirit breathes fresh upon us, we are filled with the sense of your presence everywhere. You choose not to leave us alone, but to guide us; for all your mercies we give you our thanks.

Your heavenly order conditions our decisions, O God, determining the present and future course of our lives. Your commandments ordain how we should respect other people; your judgment controls us when we seek to rebel. We pray for a recurring sense of revelation, an intrusion of perception that will enlighten our vision. We know of the Christ, how he calls us to follow. We ask for direction in our quest to obey. He calls us to struggle on behalf of your righteousness; keep us from complacency that hinders response. When we wrestle with forces that would dehumanize our neighbors, help us to be specific on what needs to occur. Give us those extraordinary glimpses of your purpose, and grant us strength to obey your will.

Help us not to be unduly anxious, when the results of our actions are not readily known. Add to our need for security a level of your providence that you promise in Christ. Chasten our desires to control our own destiny, and give us the freedom to take risks for your sake. When we stumble, set us securely once again on your path. When we take detours, keep us safe until we regain our bearings. You know who we are and where we are going. With that assurance, we shall be on our way.

ELEVENTH SUNDAY AFTER PENTECOST

Lectionary Readings for the Day
Ps. 143:1–10; Ex. 12:1–14

Rom. 8:31–39; Matt. 14:13–21

Seasonal Color:
Green

The compassion of Jesus included healing the sick and feeding the crowds. Both are a necessity in order to make others whole. While sickness attacks the body and renders it incapable of enjoying full life, hunger deprives it of nourishment so that the self is unable to grow. The size of the crowds didn't matter. With Christ the gifts of God's grace are available to all.

Call to Worship
LEADER: LORD, hear my prayer, and in your faithfulness heed my supplications; answer me in your righteousness.

RESPONSE: Teach me to do what pleases you, for you are my God; let your good Spirit lead me on level ground.

(BCP)

Prayer of Praise and Adoration
You do hear the prayers of your people, O God, and give heed to their supplications. Your faithfulness spans generations and nations, as a cloak of protection sewn with benevolent care. You promise your presence as your Spirit abides in our midst. We bow down before you, as our mothers and fathers have done before us, in praise and adoration of your gracious name.

Prayer of Confession
UNISON: O God, you teach us compassion, and we practice bigotry. You implore us to trust you, while we create idols. You send Christ as a witness that you will not forsake us; yet we fret over matters as though you cared not at all. Forgive our compulsion to control our own destiny. Look kindly upon us when we fear for our future. Have mercy upon us when we mismanage your grace. We are your people; help us to dwell in your promise.

Assurance of Pardon
LEADER: "Is it Christ Jesus, who died, yes, who was raised from the dead, who is at the right hand of God, who indeed intercedes for us?" Who then shall separate us from the love of Christ? Nothing in all of creation shall be able to separate us from the love of God in Jesus Christ. Trust in that promise!

Prayer of Dedication

O God, your compassion brings wholeness, and your forgiveness brings promise of new life. Through Christ the gifts of your grace are available to all. We place ourselves before you as recipients of your mercy; we make our offerings to you in response to Christ's call. Accept them as tributes to your glory as we dedicate ourselves anew to Christ's service.

Prayer of Thanksgiving

God of the past, the present, and the ages to come, you set the seasons, and cause the sun to rise and fall, numbering our days. The earth is yours, for you have made it. The heavens declare your handiwork; they are crafted according to your design. Streams gush from their sources to refresh us with clear waters; mighty rivers flow on their courses, as you have decreed. The seas ebb and flow and the tides are determined; waves dash against the shores of the land you created. You place us amid your ordered universe, O God, and unceasingly reveal your providential intention. If we will but dwell in the midst of your mercy, we may be assured of your benevolent protection.

So what can befall us to hinder thanksgiving? You passed over the Israelites amid their tribulation. Even today they remember your promise and care. They retell the story with glad songs as they feast. The covenant that you made you have never broken. The compassion you once showed they still observe as ordained. You sent Jesus Christ as a sign of your love. You did not spare him when he was subjected to scorn. When he died for our sins he made us the victors. When the grave could not hold him we were granted new life. He knows of our plight and how we might suffer. He prays for our well-being so that we can rejoice.

Who or what then can separate us from your love, O God? We shall continue to endure persecution. In faithfulness to Christ, we persevere in our struggle against injustice and greed. Yet even when peril or distress confronts us, we are upheld by his redeeming grace. For all you have been, are, and will continue to be, we give you thanks as we abide in your love, in the name of Christ Jesus.

TWELFTH SUNDAY AFTER PENTECOST

Lectionary Readings for the Day

Ps. 106:4–12; Ex. 14:19–31

Rom. 9:1–5; Matt. 14:22–33

Seasonal Color:
Green

Christian life is often like a storm-tossed sea. Risking the waves, we venture forth, seeking to be faithful to Christ. As he bids us to follow, the wind rises and we panic. Doubts emerge like clouds, hiding the horizon and with it the hope of reaching a haven. Then a hand reaches out with a grip of security, and assurance is given: "Have no fear."

Call to Worship

LEADER: O praise the LORD. It is good to give thanks to the LORD; for his love endures for ever.

RESPONSE: Who will tell of the LORD's mighty acts and make his praises heard?

LEADER: Happy are they who act justly and do right at all times! Let us worship God.

(NEB)

Prayer of Praise and Adoration

O God, we gather to hear of the mighty acts you perform, of how you deal justly with your people. You have led them from peril and delivered them from persecution. By the hands of Christ you lift us up to safe places, and give us a vision of how we may dwell secure in your love. Hear us now as we give thanks for your providence and praise for your mercy.

Prayer of Confession

UNISON: O God, when trials beset us it is natural to fear. Called to be courageous, we find our faith lacking. When asked to take risks, we confess our complacency. By ignoring injustice, we hope that it will subside. You have shown us how you are a God to be trusted. Leading your people, you have stayed by their side. Even Christ overcame his enemies as he hung on the cross. Forgive our reluctance to believe in your guidance, and grant us the wisdom to seek refuge in Christ.

Assurance of Pardon

LEADER: As God has driven the sea back by a strong east wind, dividing the waters and making of the sea a dry land, so now in Christ, God gives us a rock upon which to stand. Today, know that Christ is merciful and intercedes on our behalf. He is our redeemer in whom we rest forgiven.

Prayer of Dedication

O God, we go forth to serve you, wherever Christ calls us. Bless our endeavors to make his name known. May all that we do be unto your glory; the talents that we offer are the gifts of your love. As you accept us in Christ, so also acknowledge our efforts. Use what is of value to further his teachings; and what is inadequate, enhance with your grace. Hear this our prayer, O God of benevolence!

Prayer of Thanksgiving and Petition

O God of liberation, who releases the captives, hear our prayer of thanksgiving for the freedom you offer. You delivered the Israelites from the hands of the Pharaoh; you parted the seas for them to pass through. You made them aware of your presence in the pillar of fire; they knew you were near as clouds moved in the sky. When turbulent waves almost engulfed Christ's disciples, you sent your Son Jesus to calm their fears. He walked on the waters upheld by your hands and tempered their fright sustained by your mercy. We recall how Peter would walk out to greet him. He would show boldness in the midst of the tempest, only to lose heart when the seas became rough. We give you thanks for this abiding witness, which testifies to your trust in your people in spite of their doubt. We owe our very existence to your pardon, which lets us dwell in your favor. We acknowledge your safekeeping which is the bedrock of faith.

There are times when Christ calls us to take perilous journeys, to venture amid uncharted terrain in response to your will. We pray for your presence, that it will sustain us, and for your guidance, that we may not lose heart. Our cities teem with people whose lives are in torment; we need to stand with them in their trial. Jails and prisons hold countless others whose acts have been judged. We fear for our safety when we are near them, yet they, like us, are dependent on your care and in need of forgiveness. Help us to work for those measures of reform that will bring order and justice to our society. Let us speak on behalf of the defenseless, remembering Christ, who intercedes even for us. Forbid, O God, that we should take your freedom for granted, as though we have license to boast. Instead, let freedom release us to serve you with fervor, to show others that boldness which Christ taught on the cross.

THIRTEENTH SUNDAY AFTER PENTECOST

Lectionary Readings for the Day

Ps. 78:1–3, 10–20; Ex. 16:2–15   Seasonal Color:
Rom. 11:13–16, 29–32; Matt. 15:21–28   Green

A woman's daughter is healed because a mother has faith. Since the woman is a Canaanite, she is labeled a dog and unworthy of the bread of new life. Yet she is even willing to take the crumbs that happen to fall on the floor. Those who hunger and thirst after righteousness, earnestly pursuing their quest for the truth, will find adequate food to sustain them, turning to Christ in faith.

Call to Worship

LEADER: Give ear, O my people, to my teaching; incline your ears to the words of my mouth!

PEOPLE: We will tell to the coming generation the glorious deeds of the LORD and the wonders which God has wrought.

Prayer of Praise and Adoration

We broadcast your glorious deeds, O God, and spread abroad the good news of the gospel. You have not forsaken your people, but promise your presence through the gift of your Spirit. In Christ you redeem us from a past that enslaves us, and free us for a future of life lived in your love. Hear us now as we sing your praises, and fill us as we learn of your way.

Prayer of Confession

UNISON: O God, Christ calls us to faith, while we seek our own security. He teaches us to trust him, yet we don't take that risk. He expects total commitment, and we think in terms of percentage. Time after time we turn our backs on your grace, serving our idols, and forsaking our Christ. We rely on your promise in him to redeem us. We are dependent on him who can intercede for us. O God, in Christ, have mercy upon us.

Assurance of Pardon

LEADER: As God gave manna to the Israelites during their time in the wilderness, we now receive Christ as the bread of life. As God went before the Israelites as a pillar of fire, we now receive the Holy Spirit as a source of comfort and presence. God is consistently in love with those called God's people. As we are numbered among those chosen by Christ, we have assurance of God's grace and forgiveness.

Prayer of Dedication

There are those who would be glad with the crumbs from your table, O God; we have received your gifts in abundance. Make us mindful of those who are needy, as we bring you our tithes and our offerings. Use them to ease the pain of those who are suffering. As we serve others, use us to fulfill your will.

Prayer of Thanksgiving and Petition

O God of abiding presence, you stoop to hear the murmurings of your people. You do not desert them in the midst of their fears. You see that they are continually fed, and promise that they will always be led. You provide substance in the evening to sustain them through the night. With the dawn comes the promise of abundance that will last them throughout the day. We are your people, called by Christ to the banquet. You heap your mercies upon us and surround us with care. We thank you for how you watch over your children, and seek to meet their every need. Through Christ we inherit your promised deliverance, and entrust our lives to you. Hear our prayers as we make our entreaties; feed us the bread of life that Christ brings. Help us to arise refreshed with the dawn, ready to meet what awaits us.

We pray for those who are hungry, O God, those for whom the lack of food is real. The wilderness exists in their stomachs. They murmur and long to be fed. Help us to share what we have in abundance, to be good stewards over what you place in our care. Keep us from greed that inhibits our obedience, and give us compassion to respond to their needs.

We pray for those whose quest is for righteousness, who thirst after the cup of new life. They would be nourished by the commandments from heaven, and be filled by your promised redemption. Help us to tell them the good news of the gospel, how Christ died for their freedom. As we teach them what it means to obey you, let them join with us in service.

O God, keep us from taking your blessings for granted, as though we were entitled to all you give. We have what surrounds us because of your grace. In Christ's name we unceasingly praise you for your unending mercy and care.

FOURTEENTH SUNDAY AFTER PENTECOST

Lectionary Readings for the Day

Ps. 95; Ex. 17:1–7   Seasonal Color:
Rom. 11:33–36; Matt. 16:13–20   Green

Peter confesses that Jesus is the Christ, and henceforth is known as the rock upon which the church will be built. Confession has continued as a means of the faith being passed from one generation to another. It occurs during our baptism, and when we are gathered around the Lord's Table. It is a source of instruction, renewal, and commitment. It provides a solid foundation.

Call to Worship

LEADER: O come, let us sing to the LORD; let us make a joyful noise to the rock of our salvation!

RESPONSE: Let us come into God's presence with thanksgiving; let us make a joyful noise to God with songs of praise!

LEADER: O come, let us worship and bow down, let us kneel before the LORD, our Maker!

RESPONSE: For we are God's people, the flock that God shepherds. We come singing praises to the rock of salvation!

Prayer of Praise and Adoration

We give you all praise, O God of salvation. We come with devotion to you, O Christ our redeemer. We honor you, O Holy Spirit, our source of encouragement; one God who sustains us with your love and your presence. Hear our words of reverence as we bow down before you. Grace us with your presence, that we may learn of your way.

Prayer of Confession

UNISON: O God, forgive us for allowing living water to be fouled. There are times when we blame you for all our troubles, and cast upon you the waste in our lives. Our wants are insatiable through misuse of your mercy; we tap your good graces with unending requests. We let the waters of our baptism become barren and stagnant; new life cannot flourish when we don't do your will. Cleanse us through Christ, in whose name we confess our sin, and bathe us with mercy to give us fresh hope.

Assurance of Pardon

LEADER: The words of Scripture remind us that "baptism . . . now saves you, not as a removal of dirt from the body but as an appeal to God for a clear conscience, through the resurrection of Jesus Christ." Being baptized into Christ, we may approach God with assurance that Christ intercedes on our behalf.

Prayer of Dedication

O God, we confess faith in your mercy as we bring offerings before you. Use them to further your work. May our talents be useful in serving your people, and our time filled with obeying your will. The money we give is in response to your graciousness. Accept it as part of renewed commitment to Christ.

Prayer of Thanksgiving and Supplication

Who can probe the depths of your wisdom, O God, and who can attain the height of your vision? Your goodness surrounds us like the waters of the ocean. Your mercy envelops us as the sun warms our days. The gentle breezes hint of your tenderness; the claps of thunder remind us of your fierce judgment. You bring order out of chaos, command discipline in the midst of faithfulness, and offer forgiveness with the promise of new life.

You stoop to us as a mother bends to lift up her child. You lend an ear to our needs, and hear our supplications. You rejoice at the sounds of our thanksgiving, and are warmed with the songs of our praise. You leave us not alone during times of temptation, but assure us that you will be with us when put to the test. Your Spirit comforts us in our distress, and goads us to action when our commitment wanes. In Jesus you bestow on us the worth we possess; we owe all our successes to his love. He endured persecution for our sakes; he came into the world to enlighten our way.

O God, make us mindful once again of the water that cleanses. As the parched throats of the Israelites were soothed by the water that sprang from a rock, enliven our faith as we recall our baptism. May our confession of Christ as our redeemer and savior sustain us as we thirst for salvation. Lead us to offer to others the cup of hope that brings refreshment and rest. Fill our lips with the story of Christ's deliverance from evil, how he thwarted oppression with embracing love and concern. Let others through us taste your goodness, draw from the well of your wisdom, and come to confess Christ as the source of their lives.

FIFTEENTH SUNDAY AFTER PENTECOST

Lectionary Readings for the Day
Ps. 114; Ex. 19:1–9   Seasonal Color:
Rom. 12:1–13; Matt. 16:21–28   Green

The economy of the Kingdom may seem topsy-turvy to some. Something that is saved is claimed to be lost. What is forfeited on behalf of another is said to be found. What is given freely is said to be more credible than that which is earned. What is stored for tomorrow may be consumed overnight. Indeed, to follow Christ does tend to change perceptions.

Call to Worship
LEADER: Praise the LORD, all nations! Extol God, all peoples!
RESPONSE: For great is God's steadfast love toward us; and the faithfulness of the LORD endures for ever.
LEADER: Praise the LORD!

Prayer of Praise and Adoration
You are worthy of all praise, O God, more than could ever flow from our mouths. The birds sing of your glory; the day's sun rises to honor you. The mountains owe their grandeur to your design for creation; the seas have their depth, as you have decreed. We blend our voices with all your creatures, and join with your people in praising your name.

Prayer of Confession
UNISON: Forgive us, O God, when we hinder Christ's gospel. We distort the good news because we do not serve our neighbor. We seek safety rather than suffer for Christ. Our comfort comes before our confession; our allegiance is hindered, since we hide from commitment. Have mercy upon our misplaced devotion, and in Christ hear our confession as we seek to repent.

Assurance of Pardon
LEADER: The good news of the gospel is what God promised to those before us. God's covenant has been fulfilled in the raising of Jesus. Let it be known that through Jesus forgiveness of sins is proclaimed even to you. All who believe are thereby freed from their bondage. In Christ is new life for all who repent.

Prayer of Dedication

O God, we offer those gifts you bestow abundantly upon us. Take them and blend them into a composite of commitment. Empower our hands to reach out to others. Enlighten our minds to perceive clearly your will. May the money we offer support the church's endeavors, as in Christ's name we seek faithfully to respond.

Prayer of Thanksgiving and Petition

O God, you have been with your people during their affliction; you have delivered them from the bonds of oppression. As a pillar of clouds moves with the winds, your Spirit has guided your nation. You have commanded that your people be obedient; you have promised that you will not leave them; you have set your seal by making a covenant, establishing the house of Israel.

We give you thanks that by Jesus you have called us. We are your people in the household of Christ. You have endowed us with gifts in abundance, setting us apart for service, imparting whatever talents we have. You still go before us to guide us. You still expect us to follow. We praise you for your abiding presence, and faithfully seek to respond.

As a piece of fine cloth you weave us, entwining our uniqueness as individuals into a pattern of complementary expression. We thank you, O God, for the many parts of Christ's body. Keep us from judging one finer than another. Help us to work with the warp and the woof of our differences, tying each thread into a total design.

Teach us to rely on each other. With Christ as the pattern for proper behavior, may what we do be for mutual support. Replace envy with encouragement; help us to help others to grow in the faith. Save us from quarrelsome conflicts that tear down the church. May we seek always to honor opinions, and accept differences with mutual respect.

May our intentions not be conformed to this world. Rather, let them be transformed as we are renewed by your word. Lead us by your Spirit so that we discern your will, and fill us with enthusiasm to obey your commands. As you have delivered your people before us, so guide us now in the way we should go. As you have commanded them to be faithful, give us humility as we answer your call.

SIXTEENTH SUNDAY AFTER PENTECOST

Lectionary Readings for the Day
Ps. 115:1–11; Ex. 19:16–24
Rom. 13:1–10; Matt. 18:15–20

Seasonal Color:
Green

When at least two come together in God's name, God is in their midst. When they gather, there are rules for appropriate conduct. One rule deals with relationships when conflict occurs. In the church it is better to let conflict be known. There, listening occurs in the context of God's love. Perceptions may change, causing different behavior. As a result Christ's body is strengthened.

Call to Worship
LEADER: Not to us, O LORD, not to us, but to thy name ascribe the glory, for thy true love and for thy constancy.
RESPONSE: Those who fear the LORD trust in the LORD; he is their helper and their shield.
LEADER: O praise the LORD.

(NEB)

Prayer of Praise and Adoration
Your faithfulness and steadfast love surround us, O God, providing a shield against whatever would harm us. Jesus Christ has come to show us your way, and has delivered us from death to walk humbly with you. We gather this day to sing your praises and to hear your commandments. Look with favor on us as in Christ's name we pray.

Prayer of Confession
UNISON: O God, have mercy upon us when we distort your truth. At times we make idols which we serve gladly. We give to them mouths which speak words that we want to hear. They have eyes that see only what we do not hide. Their ears hear all but the secrets that we keep in our hearts. Their hands reach out only to those whom we choose. Their feet walk the paths of our making. We trust them to do whatever we command. O God, forgive us this folly of deception, and the grief that we cause you because we do not obey you.

Assurance of Pardon
LEADER: The love of God was made manifest among us, in that God sent Jesus Christ into the world, so that we might live

through Christ. In this is love, not that we loved God but that God loved us and sent the Son to be the remedy for our sins. As we receive the assurance of new life in Christ, let us also love one another.

Prayer of Dedication

"We gather together to ask the Lord's blessing; he chastens and hastens his will to make known." We do gather before you, O God, and ask that you will bless the fruits of our labor. Hasten to make your will known among us, so that all that we do shall be to your glory. Accept the gifts that we offer for the furtherance of your peace; in Christ's name we pray.

Prayer of Thanksgiving and Intercession

O God, you have chosen to speak through the mouths of your servants; by them your word has become known. The heavens shake with the roar of thunder, but you are not in the claps that are heard. The skies are lighted with the bolts of lightning, but you are not in the arcs that are seen. The air is filled with the pillars of billowing smoke, but you are not found in their density. No, you are known by the voices of those whom you have sent to serve you, who speak with the authority you give them.

We give thanks for all those who have faithfully studied your words, who through the years have made known your will. You summoned Moses and Aaron to the top of the mountain, and unto them you delivered the law. We give thanks for the prophets and poets, for the people of vision and the voices of praise. They were not afraid to take heed of your judgment, and they did not shrink from giving you the glory which you are due. We give thanks for those who have taught us, the mothers and fathers, sisters and brothers, teachers and leaders who have gone before us. We stand on their shoulders for a glimpse of your way.

In Christ your word became flesh and dwelt among us. It is in his name you call us to walk. We now seek to be faithful for his sake, as you enlist us to serve you in the decisions we make. We pray on behalf of those in authority, for leaders and representatives we have chosen to rule. Give to them proper standards for judgment and a measure of wisdom in the choices they make. Make their voices credible as they speak on behalf of the people; make their rulings in accord with what you command. You have entrusted to us the care of creation. We assign legislators to assist us as custodians of that legacy. Help them and us in Christ's name to discern your word for our day.

SEVENTEENTH SUNDAY AFTER PENTECOST

Lectionary Readings for the Day
Ps. 19:7–14; Ex. 20:1–20
Rom. 14:5–12; Matt. 18:21–35

Seasonal Color:
Green

The Lord's Table puts forgiveness in perspective. Christ invites God's people to dine. Around the table, dividing walls of hostility are breached. The peace is passed among sisters and brothers, and all partake of the bread and the fruit of the vine. As the Table remains a sign of God's reconciling love on behalf of us all, let us go forth to forgive others their debts.

Call to Worship

LEADER: The law of the LORD is perfect and revives the soul;
RESPONSE: The testimony of the LORD is sure and gives wisdom to the innocent.
LEADER: The statutes of the LORD are just and rejoice the heart;
RESPONSE: The commandment of the LORD is clear and gives light to the eyes.
LEADER: The fear of the LORD is clean and endures for ever;
RESPONSE: The judgments of the LORD are true and righteous altogether.
UNISON: Let the words of my mouth and the meditation of my heart be acceptable in your sight, O LORD, my strength and my redeemer.

(BCP)

Prayer of Confession

UNISON: O God, have mercy upon us as we make our confession. We are prone to disobedience in spite of your law. We behave foolishly in the light of your testimony. Your statutes illumine how we treat others unjustly. Your commandments reveal our wayward behavior. Afraid of your judgment if we plead our own innocence, we rely on Jesus Christ to represent us. He is our strength and the one who redeems us. Through him have mercy and forgive us our sin.

Assurance of Pardon

LEADER: As Paul has written, we do not live to ourselves alone. "If we live, we live to the Lord, and if we die, we die to the Lord; so then, whether we live or whether we die, we are the Lord's.

For to this end Christ died and lived again, that he might be Lord both of the dead and of the living." To be at one with Christ is to live in assurance that our sins are forgiven.

Prayer of Dedication

We gather about your Table, O Christ, and there partake of bread and the fruit of the vine. As bread is broken, nourish us to go forth and serve others. As the cup is passed, give us new life to proclaim equality and mercy. Accept the gifts that we offer as response to your atoning sacrifice and use them to teach others of your reconciling love.

Prayer of Thanksgiving

Your commandments, O God, are like the refiner's fire. They temper our judgment, melting down our resistance to your all-embracing will. They mold us into the people you would have us become. They reflect the brilliance of your pervasive compassion, casting shadows on our errant behavior when we stray from your path. You have taught us, O God, how we ought to behave. Your commandments revive us and set our hearts to rejoicing. They radiate the heat of your love.

You do not leave us alone in our attempts to be faithful. We give you thanks for Christ Jesus, who shows us the way. He was tempted as we are, yet did not falter. His life was blameless, his commitment complete. As he hung on the cross on behalf of our sin, the fires of sacrifice were no longer needed. He died once and for all, that we may all live. Now he intercedes for us as we offer our prayers. Through him you hear us as we dwell in his grace.

The fire that could consume us with judgment instead kindles our spirits as we stand here before you. We give you thanks for the Holy Spirit, whose counsel we seek. Through the Spirit you promise us a foretaste of heaven. We are comforted and led along paths of discipleship. Whatever decisions we are called on to make, your Spirit awaits to guide and direct our thoughts. By the Spirit we are enlivened for action and filled with the desire to serve you alone.

O God, in Christ you have taught us the meaning of obedience. May all that we do be done for his sake. Help us to extend to others the warmth of the gospel, the good news that in Christ your people are freed. Let us seek the renewal of our common life, loosing the bonds that hold millions in poverty's grasp. Set aflame in us the prophet's passion for justice so that the aim of your commandments may be fulfilled: life for all.

Lectionary Readings for the Day

Ps. 106:7–8, 19–23; Ex. 32:1–14   Seasonal Color:
Phil. 1:21–27; Matt. 20:1–16   Green

Laborers are sent into the vineyard and are told what they will be paid. The amount is the same regardless of the hours that are worked. The gifts of God's Kingdom are likewise equally allotted. They never depend upon how much one produces. The emphasis remains upon how willing we are to approach God's tasks, and not so much upon what we are due because we responded.

Call to Worship

LEADER: O praise the LORD. It is good to give thanks to the LORD; for his love endures for ever.
RESPONSE: Who will tell of the LORD's mighty acts and make his praises heard?
LEADER: Happy are they who act justly and do right at all times!

(NEB)

Prayer of Praise and Adoration

O God, if you were to mark the extent of our iniquity, who could stand before you? Yet you do not forsake us, but shower us with blessings. In Jesus Christ we receive the gift of inheritance into his household. We are called to be Christ's people, the church. We praise you; we give thanks to you; we stand to honor you, O God of redeeming grace.

A Litany of Confession

LEADER: We have sinned as our forebears did; we have done wrong and dealt wickedly.
RESPONSE: Let the manner of our life be worthy of the gospel of Christ.
LEADER: In Egypt they did not consider God's marvelous works, nor remember the abundance of God's love.
RESPONSE: Let the manner of our life be worthy of the gospel of Christ.
LEADER: Israel made a bull-calf at Horeb and worshiped a molten image.
RESPONSE: Let the manner of our life be worthy of the gospel of Christ.

LEADER:	So they exchanged their glory for the image of an ox that feeds on grass.
RESPONSE:	Let the manner of our life be worthy of the gospel of Christ.
LEADER:	They forgot God their Savior, who had done great things in Egypt.
RESPONSE:	Let the manner of our life be worthy of the gospel of Christ.
LEADER:	May I hear that you stand firm in one spirit, with one mind striving side by side for the faith of the gospel.
RESPONSE:	Let the manner of our life be worthy of the gospel of Christ.

Prayer of Dedication

O God, you give us tasks to perform. You equip us with strengths and abilities beyond what we deserve. In Christ you call us to faithfulness, to exercise obedience, to be deliberate in our discipline. We come now offering to you the results of our labors. Use them as a means to further your work in Christ's name.

Prayer of Thanksgiving

O God, you called a people to give you their praise. You made a covenant with them, sealing it with an oath. You kept your promises through the ages, showing to all that you are the God we can trust. Yet your wrath was kindled when your people turned to idols; your glory you will not share with another. In spite of their sin you forsook not your intentions; your presence remained as a source of their hope.

In Christ you have called us to be responsible disciples, to do work that befits your redemption. Our vineyards are the scenes of the diverse tasks in church and community. In halls and assemblies where decisions are debated, in libraries where study occurs, on pavements that resound with footsteps and movement, your people are alert to your call to obey.

We thank you for those who appear often in public, leaders and entertainers whose faces we know. We give thanks also for countless who are nameless, whose tasks make our days more enjoyable. We thank you for their continuing diligence. May the products of all these efforts never become substitutes for you, O God. Let them rather be received as gifts and used to further Christ's vision of the redeemed society.

NINETEENTH SUNDAY AFTER PENTECOST

Lectionary Readings for the Day
Ps. 99; Ex. 33:12–23
Phil. 2:1–13; Matt. 21:28–32

Seasonal Color:
Green

Followers of Christ are sent to work in the vineyard. Will they respond or evade the call? If they say yes, then action is implied. Christ offers repentance to those who hold back, while those who say yes then fail to act are judged. Relationship with Christ demands that our actions match our intentions.

Call to Worship
LEADER: The LORD is great in Zion; [God] is high above all peoples.

RESPONSE: Let [us] confess [God's] Name, which is great and awesome; [God] is the Holy One.

(BCP)

Prayer of Praise and Adoration
O God, your grandeur towers above the highest peaks; your strength can make them tremble and fall. Your love is deeper than the valleys of the oceans, and as encompassing as the waters that cover the earth. In Christ Jesus you call us your children and through him your word is forever made known. Be with us now as in Christ's name we gather. Accept our praises as we confess him Redeemer and Lord.

Prayer of Confession
UNISON: God of compassion, have mercy upon us as we make our confession. How often we do not do what we intended! What we confess is not how we act. We hear your word preached and we give our assent, but faith is found wanting when it comes time to obey. We are confronted by conflict; decisions are called for. Our desires are at odds with what you command, and we default on our promise to you. O Christ, have mercy upon us and strengthen us so that we can be trusted as you are.

Assurance of Pardon
LEADER: Again, hear the words of Paul when he writes that God has bestowed on Christ "the name which is above every name, that at the name of Jesus every knee should bow . . . and every tongue confess that Jesus Christ is Lord." As we make our confes-

sion we have the assurance that the exalted Christ intercedes on our behalf.

Prayer of Dedication

As we are called to be faithful in our work, O God, accept our gifts as we seek to respond. May our hearts be as willing as your grace is reassuring. May our faith be as firm as your forgiveness that frees us. May our decisions be as deliberate as your righteousness that delivers us. You have called us your own, O Christ. We confess you as Lord of all that we have and all that we are.

Prayer of Thanksgiving

O God, you are not hidden from us, but cause yourself to be known. By your mighty deeds you led your people from danger to safety. Still waters were a source for refreshment, a cleft of the rock gave firmness for footing. There is not a day that goes by that you reveal not your wishes. You undergird us with mercy, and your grace gives us hope.

We give you thanks for all those who surround us. They reveal your love as they offer guidance. Their hands reach out to lift us from our depths of despair. They are not hesitant when we ask for assistance. Their voices are soothing as they speak words that encourage us.

We give thanks for those moments when we are made aware of your kindness. You temper your judgment with patience. You give us the cup to refresh our bodies; you give us bread daily to nurture our growth. Our baptism is a sign that we are heirs of the covenant. All our senses are made aware of your grace.

We give you thanks for Christ Jesus, whose Spirit abides with us constantly. Even when we would hide from you we are left not alone. We are assured of your presence when we face danger; you give us wisdom which keeps us from falling. Our days have new meaning since Christ intercedes for us. We dwell with a confidence that we receive by Christ's call.

O God, make known your will in the decisions that face us. Surrounded by such a significant witness, may we not shrink from our commitment to serve. We confess anew that in you alone abides our hope of salvation. With Christ to guide us we set forth on our tasks.

Lectionary Readings for the Day

Ps. 81:1–10; Num. 27:12–23   Seasonal Color:
Phil. 3:12–21; Matt. 21:33–43   Green

The stone which the builders rejected becomes the corner upon which the structure is built. Stones from the past have a way of providing foundations in the present. Even those at first rejected are appreciated in time. Confessions and creeds, which have withstood the ages, may be tempered and worn; but they likewise remain as foundations of our faith.

Call to Worship

LEADER: Listen, my people, while I give you a solemn charge. I am the LORD your God who brought you up from Egypt.

RESPONSE: Sing out in praise of God our refuge, acclaim the God of Jacob.

(NEB)

Prayer of Praise and Adoration

All praise be unto you, O God, maker of heaven and earth. You cause the day to dawn with the promise of new life; you watch over us through the night, giving us rest from our labors. Fill us now with the presence of your Holy Spirit, so that what we say proclaims your glory, and what we do reflects your will, through Christ our redeemer, in whose name we gather.

Prayer of Confession

UNISON: O God, have mercy upon us as we confess our sin. We live as enemies of the cross when we crave earthly things, glory in the weakness of others, yearn above all for satisfaction for ourselves, and serve only those gods who do what we want. Having attained the prize of your mercy in Jesus, help us to obey him as the source of new life.

Assurance of Pardon

LEADER: As the Gospel reminds us, "The very stone which the builders rejected has become the head of the corner; this was the Lord's doing, and it is marvelous in our eyes." Christ is our foundation; God's will in him cannot be shaken. Our redemption is sure; we are forgiven.

Prayer of Dedication

We rely on your promise, O God, that you will not forsake us; our pledge to you is that we will be faithful. As we stand on the shoulders of those who have gone before, give us a vision of what commitment can mean. Accept the gifts that we place here before you, as we in our day make our response. Let what we do be an example for others so that future believers learn of Christ and his way.

Prayer of Thanksgiving and Supplication

O God, you gave your people a vision of the promised land. You went before them as a pillar of cloud by day and a pillar of fire by night. Your power was as great as you have promised; yet you were slow to anger, and forgave iniquity. Your glory then has not faded today. Amid the novelties of every age you provide a constancy of righteousness in Christ Jesus.

From age to age you have chosen leaders from among your people. They have been granted insight into your encompassing will. We give you thanks for their commitment and praise you for their insight. We have been taught by them. May we never forget this precious legacy as we in our time respond to your call.

We give you thanks for creeds and confessions, declarations from the church's past that give us a glimpse of courage and obedience. They were honed and tempered by the experience of our ancestors in faith, as they were led by the Spirit through their wilderness. Led by the same Spirit, help us to learn from these testaments of faith, and to use them wisely as we seek to interpret Christ's word for this age.

Set upon the stage of our history, we seek to play our part in the continuing reformation of the church. Help us freely to accept Christ's call to perform in the drama of our time, and to develop our assigned role with skill and sensitivity. We need your guidance as we interpret Scripture. We pray for discipline as we endeavor to learn our lines well. Bind us together as a cast of believers supporting one another in growth.

When the reviews of our acts are written in a generation to come, may we be found to have met the challenge well. With Christ as our prompter, help us to unfold the drama of salvation that is filled with the glory and praise of your righteousness.

TWENTY-FIRST SUNDAY AFTER PENTECOST

Lectionary Readings for the Day
Ps. 135:1–14; Deut. 34:1–12
Phil. 4:1–9; Matt. 22:1–14

Seasonal Color:
Green

The wedding feast was prepared; the invitations had been sent. But some guests would not come. Others made light of the feast by insisting they were too busy, or otherwise engaged. When the Lord's Table is spread, the call is extended. All those are welcome who confess their faith in Jesus Christ. God's chosen people shall partake of the heavenly banquet.

Call to Worship
LEADER: Give praise, you that stand in the house of the LORD, in the courts of the house of our God!
RESPONSE: God is gracious and good. We shall praise the Lord, and sing to God's name.

(Author's paraphrase)

Prayer of Praise and Adoration
Whatever is true, whatever is honorable, whatever is just, whatever is pure, whatever is lovely, whatever is gracious, all, O God, are gifts of your grace. We gather to sing praises unto your name, and to extol your virtues in the midst of our neighbors. Your commandments are just; they give us direction. Your covenant is encompassing, as in Christ we are knit together. All honor is yours as we rejoice in your glory!

Prayer of Confession
UNISON: O Christ, we confess that we too make light of your invitation. We are reluctant to come when the feast is made ready. Our time is committed; business is pressing. We are afraid we will be with the wrong people. At times dissension hinders our response. We are not at peace with those likewise invited. We are in need of forgiveness to heal our divisions, and a measure of mercy to partake of your grace.

Assurance of Pardon
LEADER: Scripture reminds us that the bread of God is that which comes down from heaven, and gives life to the world. Jesus has taught that he is the bread of life. Whoever lives and believes

in Jesus Christ as the bread of life has eternal life; therein abides our assurance of pardon and renewal.

Prayer of Dedication

O God, you call us to be agents of Christ's way. We accept the commission as we confess faith in his will. What we now offer reflects our commitment. Accept our labors as befitting your righteousness. Enhance our endeavors by sending your Spirit. May our obedience be worthy of your continuing trust.

Prayer of Thanksgiving and Petition

O God, you know our inmost thoughts before the words cross our lips. Your wisdom embraces the seen and the unseen. Your judgment probes to the core of our being. Your love extends beyond the farthest reaches of the oceans. The highest peaks of the mountains do not approach the heights of your compassion. You are God whose anger is kindled by injustice, whose heart is touched by the suffering of a child. Your grace extends to those who bow down and worship your name; you have sent Christ as a means of salvation to all who believe. We give you thanks, O God, that in him you look with favor upon us. Cleanse the thoughts of our hearts by the inspiration of your Holy Spirit, that we may be found acceptable in your sight, our strength and redeemer.

We pray that we shall stand firm in the face of tribulation. May our conviction not waver as we witness in Christ's name. When we are tossed to and fro by the trials that beset us, give us clear heads and open hearts so that we can hear what you are saying. As we confront contemporary demons that tempt us from your way, keep us resolute in Christ's own triumph over the destructive power of evil.

We pray for boldness to risk greater ventures, to take specific steps in response to your love. Give us the sense to recognize evil, and the courage to oppose it. As Christ was released from the tomb that bound him, may we too be freed from powers that impede us. Lift us to the heights where we can gain a vision of your eternal order; then set us in the midst of those who need a glimpse of your peace.

TWENTY-SECOND SUNDAY AFTER PENTECOST

Lectionary Readings for the Day
Ps. 146; Ruth 1:1–19a
I Thess. 1:1–10; Matt. 22:15–22

Seasonal Color:
Green

The distinction is made between what is God's and what is Caesar's. The decision remains, who shall be served? If it be God, then God's will shall be done. If it be Caesar, then Caesar shall reign. Idolatry occurs when the distinction is blurred. When put to the test, Jesus simply asks the question: to whom will allegiance be given?

Call to Worship
LEADER: O praise the LORD. Praise the LORD, my soul.
RESPONSE: As long as I live I will praise the LORD; I will sing psalms to my God all my life long.

(NEB)

Prayer of Praise and Adoration
All of our lives are full of your mercy, O God; wherever we turn you are sure to be there. If we are found in the depths of depression, you lift up our spirits with the hope of new life. When we bound to the heights of ecstasy, you rejoice with us and make our feet light. You surround us with your Spirit who knows our needs before we announce them. We give you all praise, O God of all life.

Prayer of Confession
UNISON: O God, distinctions become blurred when we are called on to serve you. We have been taught that to serve you is to obey you; at times fidelity to others gets in our way. Societal pressures appeal to that sense of security that speaks to our welfare. Mores and customs become mandates; higher loyalties are put aside. O God, we confess our mixed allegiance. Have mercy upon us as we face obligations, and reclaim us from error when we obey not your will.

Assurance of Pardon
LEADER: Remember the words of the prophet Jeremiah when he wrote: "Behold, the days are coming, says the LORD, when . . . I will put my law within them, and I will write it upon their hearts; and I will be their God, and they shall be my people . . . ; for I

will forgive their iniquity, and I will remember their sin no more."
Therein lies our assurance.

Prayer of Dedication

O God, we hear about the cost of discipleship. Nothing less than our whole life is required. We dedicate these gifts in response to Christ's call, and offer ourselves in full commitment. Take us and mold us according to his will. We pray that who we are may be acceptable, what we do may find favor, and that which we give will reflect your love.

Prayer of Intercession

O God, you were with Naomi in her time of sorrow. Orpah and Ruth also knew of your love. You have heard the weeping of those sorely afflicted; you have felt the need of those too weak to speak. We give you thanks, O God, for your tender compassion, how you watch over your people with care. We give you thanks that in Christ you have shown us your mercy; filled with his Spirit we make our needs known before you. Hear us now as we intercede on behalf of those who have no advocates. Be with them in their time of tribulation.

We pray for all those imprisoned for whatever cause. As Christ broke the fetters of death that closed in about him, may those who are confined be freed by his love. Let us care enough to work for humane systems of justice, to advocate means whereby healing occurs. Keep us, O God, from making too hasty judgments, from casting aside as unwanted those Christ came to redeem.

We pray on behalf of those for whom hope is a fantasy, the forlorn and forgotten who now seem so alone. Comfort those who through death have lost a loved one, or for reasons unknown could never count on a friend. Help us to reach out to them in their plight, and to embrace them in tenderness. As Christ was quick to lift the wounded, may we too be instant in transmitting his kindness.

We pray on behalf of those who hunger and thirst after righteousness, for whom society seems like an alien place. May they through Christ find dignity, and learn of his reign which offers new life. Help us, O God, to declare to them as to us the day of deliverance. Help us to offer the bread and the cup by which we are nourished as a source of sustenance for all those who yearn for a taste of your mercy.

TWENTY-THIRD SUNDAY AFTER PENTECOST

Lectionary Readings for the Day
Ps. 128; Ruth 2:1–13

I Thess. 2:1–8; Matt. 22:34–46

Seasonal Color:
Green

Obedience to God is both a gift and a task. The heart has been given the ability to love. The soul has been freed from the finality of death. The mind has been granted the inspiration of God's Spirit. God has bestowed means whereby we may return God's love. Our task is to place ourselves, so endowed, in service to others—that they too may know of God's mercy and grace.

Call to Worship
LEADER: Happy is every one who fears God, and follows the ways of the Lord!

RESPONSE: You shall eat the fruit of the labor of your hands; you shall be happy, and it shall be well with you.

LEADER: Let us worship God.

(Author's paraphrase)

Prayer of Praise and Adoration
The works of our hands are gifts of your mercy, O God, and all that we have are signs of your love. If we have strength, it is because you uplift us; when we have joy, it is on account of your grace. We praise you when you comfort us. We are afraid when you judge us in anger. With Christ to intercede, accept now our worship. May it be worthy of the care you show us.

Litany of Confession
LEADER: We are taught to love you, O God, with all of our heart;

RESPONSE: We confess that our allegiance is less than complete.

LEADER: We are taught to love you, O God, with all of our soul;

RESPONSE: We confess that we long to have our own way.

LEADER: We are taught to love you, O God, with all of our mind;

RESPONSE: We confess that our thoughts are seldom so pure.

LEADER: We are taught to love neighbors as we love ourselves;

RESPONSE: We confess preference for ourselves being first.

LEADER: God have mercy upon us as we make our confession.
RESPONSE: Christ have mercy upon us and forgive our sin.

Assurance of Pardon
LEADER: In Christ the "fulness of God was pleased to dwell, and through him to reconcile to himself all things, . . . making peace by the blood of his cross." Know that in Christ you have been reconciled so that through him you are presented holy and blameless to God. Therein lies our assurance of pardon.

Prayer of Dedication
O God, you call us as stewards to take care of your creation. As we till its soil, help us also to replenish and nurture the earth. As we sow seeds for tomorrow's crops, teach us the meaning of patience and hope. As we reap the harvest, guide us to see that all your people are fed.

Prayer of Thanksgiving and Supplication
O God, as you looked with favor on your daughter Ruth, so in all ages you have blessed your children. The fruits of your goodness have made glad your people; gleanings of the harvest have reflected your grace. When with fear and trembling your followers have faced an unknown future, you have sent forth your Spirit to comfort their plight. We thank you, O God, that your presence abides with us. We rejoice in the truth which Christ died to make known. We pray with the assurance that you know our anxieties.

We pray for patience when we experience conflict. Help us take the time necessary to discern your will. When we are hemmed in on every side, and we must decide, give us boldness to act, and a clear sense of your guidance as we move out.

Control our tempers, O God, when we feel put down. As once and for all Christ died to redeem us, may we save others from suffering disgrace. Keep us humble in the face of our enemies, armed with the conviction that your love abides. Help us to honor their need for well-being, and work for reconciliation.

We pray for courage in declaring the gospel. Help us not to hide the faith we confess. May others see sincerity in how we seek solutions, and honesty in our confrontation with forces that oppose your will. As you call us in Christ's name to specific tasks of ministry, give us strength to respond with insight and hope. Send the Spirit to guide us as we go forth to serve.

TWENTY-FOURTH SUNDAY AFTER PENTECOST

Lectionary Readings for the Day
Ps. 127; Ruth 4:7–17
I Thess. 2:9–13, 17–20; Matt. 23:1–12

Seasonal Color:
Green

"Whoever exalts himself will be humbled, and whoever humbles himself will be exalted." To exalt or humble is to position one's self in relationship to another. Christ calls his followers to be servants since there is only one master. Let us then be in a position to serve the other person. For then the other's needs and concerns will be raised above our own and Christ will be faithful in meeting our needs.

Call to Worship
LEADER: If Yahweh does not build the house, in vain the masons toil;

RESPONSE: If Yahweh does not guard the city, in vain the sentries watch. *(JB)*

LEADER: But you, O God, in Christ establish the church and in his name we gather.

RESPONSE: And by your Spirit you watch over your people, giving us cause to rejoice.

(Author's paraphrase)

Prayer of Praise and Adoration
You have built your house on a rock, O God, and have sent us the Christ as its cornerstone. We praise your name for the assurance Christ gives us, and rejoice in the hope that his presence provides. Bring now your Spirit into the midst of our gathering and bless our endeavors as we follow Christ's call. May our voices be blended into one of thanksgiving and our actions united into one of great praise.

Prayer of Confession
UNISON: O God, have mercy upon us as we make our confession. So often what we preach is not what we practice. We ourselves do not bear the burdens we impose on others. We expect commendation for our acts of benevolence; we like others to see us and how well we behave. Titles and honors are worn with pride, sometimes with envy, when others about us seem to be getting ahead. O God, forgive our craving to be exalted; help us to be humble in the knowledge that we live by grace alone.

Assurance of Pardon

LEADER: Remember Jesus Christ, "who, though he was in the form of God, did not count equality with God a thing to be grasped, but emptied himself, taking the form of a servant." He bore our sins on a cross that we might die to sin and rise to life anew. In Christ we boast of the good news of God's love.

Prayer of Dedication

You are witness, O God, to the work we do for the sake of Christ Jesus. To your name is all honor due. Take the gifts that we bring, and bless our endeavors to be faithful. Use us to lead others to the truth of your gospel.

Prayer of Thanksgiving and Supplication

O God of all wisdom, the truth of your love is like a rare treasure: its value exceeds comprehension and its scope is beyond the farthest limits of our imagination. To grasp it for a moment is to be lifted high above whatever may threaten us; to be nurtured by it is to be held in an embrace that protects us from ultimate harm. Your truth leads us along the way of life that develops discipleship, challenging our vision which is self-centered and helping us to focus on your commands and desires. It breeds acts of compassion, causing steps to be taken that will bring justice to light. It holds within it hope for tomorrow, and puts in perspective the toil of today.

We give you thanks for Christ Jesus, who makes your love known. It is through him that we claim our inheritance, and participate in the promise of a day without end. As he taught his disciples what it means to serve others, so also we learn how we ought to live. As he sacrificed himself on the cross for our salvation, so also we know that we may suffer abuse. As the grave could not hold him, since he dwells by your side, so also our foes will not harm us, since we abide by your grace.

O God, as we reaffirm our confession in Christ our redeemer, help us to pass on to others the truth of your love. May we be for them a treasure trove of understanding and acceptance, so that they can discover the wealth of your blessings. We pray for guidance as we act out Christ's gospel, for each individual has a particular need to be met. Help us to treat your people as unique sisters and brothers. Help us to make the most of unexpected opportunities to share your benevolent mercy and care, so that others are led to confess you as their God.

TWENTY-FIFTH SUNDAY AFTER PENTECOST

Lectionary Readings for the Day
Ps. 50:7–15; Amos 5:18–24
I Thess. 4:13–18; Matt. 25:1–13

Seasonal Color:
Green

As we approach the season of Advent, we read: "Watch therefore, for you know neither the day nor the hour." How strange, when everyone knows the date of Christmas! May our calendars, however, not limit our preparation for the usual, and our anticipation of the day rule out God's surprises.

Call to Worship
LEADER: Offer to God the sacrifice of thanksgiving and pay your vows to the Most High. *(NEB)*

RESPONSE: And what does God require from us, but that we let justice roll down like waters, and righteousness like an everlasting stream.

Prayer of Praise and Adoration
O God, your justice is like the waters that cleanse us from all inequity, your righteousness like streams of goodness washing our soul. You purify the thoughts of our minds by the inspiration of your Holy Spirit, and sanctify our actions by the gift of your Son Jesus Christ. We appear now before you as children renewed by your mercy, to give you all praise in response to your grace.

Prayer of Confession
LEADER: I hate, I despise your feasts.

RESPONSE: O God, forgive our gluttony and greed.

LEADER: I take no delight in your solemn assemblies.

RESPONSE: O God, forgive our unwillingness to rejoice in the gospel.

LEADER: Even though you offer me your burnt offerings and cereal offerings, I will not accept them.

RESPQNSE: O God, forgive our lack of total commitment.

LEADER: The peace offerings of your fatted beasts I will not look upon.

RESPONSE: O God, forgive our hesitancy to seek reconciliation.

LEADER: Take away from me the noise of your songs.

RESPONSE: O God, forgive our reluctance to listen when you speak.

LEADER: To the melody of your harps I will not listen.

O God, have mercy upon us and hear our confession. As your justice rolls down upon us, may your righteousness cleanse us from all of our sin.

Assurance of Pardon

LEADER: Paul delivers words of comfort when he writes, "May the God of peace . . . sanctify you wholly; and may your spirit and soul and body be kept sound and blameless at the coming of our Lord Jesus Christ." God who calls you is faithful, and God will do it. Peace be with you.

Prayer of Dedication

O God, we offer our prayers of thanksgiving. Words of praise and adoration are your due. You take no delight in solemn assemblies; peace offerings and burnt offerings you do not want yet accept what we give as signs of our promise to be faithful.

Prayer of Thanksgiving

God of infinite mercy, we offer thanksgiving for your goodness. You have not forsaken your people. When our tables are laden, it is due to your grace. Our lungs are filled with the life you breathe into us; our limbs move with purpose because of the strength you impart. When anxieties engulf us, you hide not your compassion. If we are afflicted with pain, you comfort us with your presence.

We give you thanks for Christ Jesus, who fulfills all that you promised. In him we have confidence that you accept who we are. It is he who redeems us in spite of our rebellion, and offers salvation when we stray from your will. He tempers your judgment with his intercession, and stays your anger as he acts on our behalf. We can approach you with assurance that in Christ you will hear us, and we take heart that we still dwell in your favor.

We give thanks for our loved ones who are at rest now with you. Their faith in Christ Jesus helped transform our lives. We thank you as well for prophets and saints of all ages. Their journeys taken in obedience have inspired us to pilgrimage. We thank you for all those who have shown us how to seek justice and kindness. By their example our lives have perspective, and because of their commitment, we too have had faith. As we continue our own quest to be obedient, help us to remember your presence throughout history.

TWENTY-SIXTH SUNDAY AFTER PENTECOST

Lectionary Readings for the Day
Ps. 76; Zeph. 1:7, 12–18
I Thess. 5:1–11; Matt. 25:14–30

Seasonal Color:
Green

The parable of the talents is a classic reminder that we are stewards of all the creation. We are not to hoard its goods, nor hurt and destroy it. It is ours to return when the master comes to settle accounts. What we have to give will depend upon how we care for it, multiply its fruits, and sustain its yield. To be faithful even over a little is to be given responsibility for much.

Call to Worship
LEADER: Be silent before God. For the day of Yahweh is near.
RESPONSE: Yes, Yahweh has prepared a sacrifice, and has consecrated the guests.
LEADER: Fulfill the promises you make to Yahweh your God.
RESPONSE: The great day of Yahweh is near; near, and coming with speed.

(Author's paraphrase)

Prayer of Praise and Adoration
Your day, O God, draws near with deliberate haste. We prepare ourselves for the providence that you promise to us in Christ. As we gather in this place to give you all praise and glory, fill us so with the Holy Spirit that we may discern your will. May we thereby be led to worship you in all that we do, with thanksgiving to Jesus, who shows us the way.

Prayer of Confession
UNISON: O God, have mercy upon us as we confess our sin. Christ calls us stewards, but we squander your gifts. He gives us tasks to perform, yet we do as we please. He sends us to minister on behalf of those suffering; we are slow to respond until our own needs are met. He expects us to praise you in all that we do; we take all the credit for those things we do well. Forgive us and help us to be more obedient.

Assurance of Pardon
LEADER: Paul reminds us that, "since we belong to the day, let us be sober, and put on the breastplate of faith and love, and for a helmet the hope of salvation. For God has not destined us for

wrath, but to obtain salvation through our Lord Jesus Christ." Therein abides our assurance of pardon.

Prayer of Dedication

O God, you endow us with talent beyond what we earn or deserve. You seek from us service to you in all that we think, yearn for, and do. As we bring our gifts and offerings before you, may they reflect a wise investment of your trust in us. May their yield continue to abound as the work that we do spreads your will farther.

Prayer of Thanksgiving and Supplication

O God of all times and all seasons, great and wonderful are all your works. You set the sun in the heavens to give warmth to our days. The moon and the stars you cause to light up the night. We spend our days surrounded by your abiding presence; our nights are filled with the assurance that you care for the whole of creation. When we awake, we arise refreshed from the sleep that you grant us. When we retire, we rest secure in the comfort that you provide.

As shadows lengthen and daylight hours grow shorter, praise of your name still comes forth from our mouths. You are God for all seasons of our lives. When winter chills us, you warm us with your love. With the appearance of springtime, you cause new life to abound. The long days of summer you fill with times of recreation and leisure. During the fall, we thank you for the yield that comes forth from the earth.

Teach us, O God, so to number our days that all that we do may be done in response to your grace. As you sent us the Christ to redeem us from darkness, may we live in obedience to your will as the children of light. Give us the insight to discern your word, and the conviction to act according to what Christ commands us to do.

As you send us the Spirit as proof of your abiding goodness, may we be courageous in how we care for creation. May the love we show our sisters and brothers open their eyes to the dawn of new life. Help us in the midst of trials to be made bold by the confession that Christ stands with us. May we rise above everyday living to catch sight of your wonderful works and never fear the involvement that a new day can bring. You are God of the harvest; we offer ourselves in response to your providence.

TWENTY-SEVENTH SUNDAY AFTER PENTECOST
CHRIST THE KING

Lectionary Readings for the Day
Ps. 23; Ezek. 34:11–16, 20–24   Seasonal Color:
I Cor. 15:20–28; Matt. 25:31–46   White

God judges obedience by how well the needs of others are met. When they hunger and thirst, where is the bread of new life? When they are outcast or imprisoned, what has become of Christ's compassion and care? When they are sick or alone, how are they told of the miracles Jesus performed? As the least of God's people are raised to behold the hope of the gospel, God's will is done.

Call to Worship
LEADER: The LORD is my shepherd; I shall not be in want.
RESPONSE: You spread a table before me in the presence of those who trouble me;
LEADER: You have anointed my head with oil, and my cup is running over.
RESPONSE: Surely your goodness and mercy shall follow me all the days of my life,
LEADER: And I will dwell in the house of the LORD for ever.
                                           (BCP)

Prayer of Praise and Adoration
O God, you have given us Christ, who shepherds the church. He is the host when the table is spread. We praise your name for all the goodness you give us, the mercy which, like oil, anoints all of our lives. As we dwell secure in the sanctuary of your salvation, open to us the truth of your word. Lead us to serve you more faithfully as in Christ you have called us to do your will.

Litany of Affirmation
LEADER: For as in Adam all die, so also in Christ shall all be made alive.
RESPONSE: In fact Christ has been raised from the dead, the first fruits of those who have fallen asleep.
LEADER: But each in order: Christ the first fruits, then at his coming those who belong to Christ.
RESPONSE: In fact Christ has been raised from the dead, the first fruits of those who have fallen asleep.

LEADER:	Then comes the end, when he delivers the kingdom to God after destroying every rule and every authority and power.
RESPONSE:	That God may be everything to every one.
LEADER:	For Christ must reign until he has put all his enemies under his feet.
RESPONSE:	That God may be everything to every one.
LEADER:	The last enemy to be destroyed is death.
RESPONSE:	That God may be everything to every one.

Prayer of Dedication

O God, may your will be done as the least of your children are led to behold the hope of the gospel. Take our lives and let them be consecrated to obeying what Christ commands. Take our gifts and use them as means of hope to those who hunger and thirst after righteousness. Take our time and fill it with a sense of your abiding Spirit, that others may learn of your redeeming grace.

Prayer of Thanksgiving and Petition

Shepherd God of Israel, who sent Jesus to be the shepherd of the church, we thank you for his love which guides and nurtures your people. He cradles us in his arms and brings us back to the fold and to safety. He leads us to pastures where quiet streams flow. In the waters of baptism we are made members of his fold. In the breaking of bread we are strengthened; the cup passed among us is the sign of new life. The old find consolation; the young are granted visions.

We thank you that we are numbered as the flock of Jesus, the Good Shepherd. He names us as he calls us to walk with him. He leads us on the journey our life will take as his followers; he teaches us what it means to obey. By his judgment we will know when we have strayed; by his mercy we will be saved from foolish ways.

By your mercy, teach us the meaning of true righteousness. Help us to know what it means to serve your people in need. Where there is hunger, let us be the ones to offer bread. When others thirst, let us offer the cup of cold water in Christ's name. Through us may the stranger find a place to stay, and the tattered and the naked be clothed. May our ministry serve as the keys to your Kingdom, unlocking the gates so that your people enter the sheepfold. There may all find shelter and grow in faith and obedience as followers of Him who fulfilled all of your will.

Index of Scripture Readings